T0208341

THE WELL ETERNAL

Reflections on Messiah

Daniel Thomas
(Introduction by Jerome A. Henry)

BALBOA.
PRESS

A DIVISION OF HAY HOUSE

Scripture taken from the New King James Version®. Copyright © 1982 by Thomas Nelson. Used by permission. All rights reserved.

Balboa Press books may be ordered through booksellers or by contacting:

Balboa Press
A Division of Hay House
1663 Liberty Drive
Bloomington, IN 47403
www.balboapress.com
1 (877) 407-4847

Print information available on the last page.

ISBN: 978-1-9822-3077-7 (sc)
ISBN: 978-1-9822-3079-1 (hc)
ISBN: 978-1-9822-3078-4 (e)

Library of Congress Control Number: 2019909238

Balboa Press rev. date: 08/29/2019

PREFACE

Message in a bottle

I love the idea of sending a message in a bottle. I have always wanted to write something on a piece of plain white paper, roll it up, slip it into a bottle and let the ocean's currents take it away to a far away land. Safe inside the confines of the glass bottle, the words would travel through time and vast oceanic expanses. After many months or years, the bottle would wash up onto the shore and eventually into someone's hands.

How exciting it would be to find that bottle and read the contents of the note contained inside. Now suppose the writer of the note was a President, a King or what if the message came from outside of our world, beyond time and space, wouldn't you be interested in reading it?

The fact is that we have a message just like that. The bible is a love letter from our Creator. What a treasure we have at our fingertips and what a tragedy if we never discover the wisdom contained inside. "All Scripture is given by inspiration of God, and is profitable for doctrine, for reproof, for correction, for instruction in righteousness, that the man of God may be complete, thoroughly equipped for every good work." 2 Timothy 3:16. NKJV

I talk to people who say they don't believe in God. They give me all sorts of reasons for their lack of faith but basically it comes down to the absence of solid evidence. Although misguided, they are in good company. Even one of Jesus' disciples, Thomas, said "Unless I see in His hands the print of the nails, and put my finger into the print of the nails, and put my hand into His side, I will not believe." John 20:25. NKJV

There are many infallible proofs for God's existence, all of which are found inside the pages of the bible. "So then faith comes by hearing, and hearing by the word of God." Romans 10:17 NKJV. But unless we open and hear the word, the seeds of faith can't be planted in our hearts. All faith takes is a seed, some water and some warm light from the Son.

Found near the end of the New Testament, is the book of Hebrews. Chapter eleven is called the "Hall of faith". There in verse 1 we find the definition of faith "Now faith is the substance of things hoped for, the evidence of things not seen." It's also said that without faith it's impossible to please God.

We're told Abel offered to God a more excellent sacrifice than Cain by offering up a lamb from the flock. God had instructed that our sin can only be covered up with blood. "And according to the law almost all things are purified with blood, and without the shedding of blood there is no remission of sin". Hebrews 9:22. NKJV

Noah who had never seen one drop of rain, by faith built an ark to God's specifications and saved his household of eight. The only people who did not perish in the worldwide deluge were the people who were safely on the ark.

Once they were inside, it was God who shut the door and condemned the entire lost world outside.

On faith Abraham left his homeland and journeyed to a land he had never seen before. Even when God asked him to sacrifice his only son, Isaac, Abraham obeys and witnesses grace and mercy as God delivers Isaac from certain death by providing a ram caught in the thicket. Later on, it would happen that on that very same mountain, Moriah, God would provide His one and only son to become our sacrifice.

So God did send us a message but it was not hidden inside of a bottle. Instead, He carefully inspired men to record ahead of time foretelling what was going to happen in the future. Then through the blood of many martyrs, the books were canonized, published and distributed worldwide.

One day Jesus will return as the King of kings and the Lord of lords to shepherd His people and put an end to sin. At that time all of us who have put our trust in Him, will rejoice as the Lamb of God takes the scroll and breaks its seals, redeeming the earth.

"Therefore we also, since we are surrounded by so great a cloud of witnesses, let us lay aside every weight, and the sin which so easily ensnares us, and let us run with endurance the race that is set before us, looking unto Jesus, the author and finisher of our faith, who for the joy that was set before Him endured the cross, despising the shame, and has set down at the right hand of the throne of God." Hebrews 12:1, 2 NKJV

CONTENTS

INTRODUCTION

THE WELL ETERNAL draws from the Source that never runs dry; an effervescent ever-flowing water (Spirit) supply.

> *"If anyone thirsts, let him come to Me and drink. He who believes in Me, as the Scripture has said, out of his heart will flow rivers of living water." (John 7: 37)*

The Word Ladder

Hebrew sages believed that God, the Creator of Heaven and earth, used elements of His Holy Name (YHVH) to create "all there is and ever will be."

In the Gospel of John, we read,

> *"In the beginning the Word already existed. The Word was with God; and the Word was God. He was already with God in the beginning. Everything came into existence through Him. He (the Word) was the source of life; and that life was light for humanity. The light that darkness cannot extinguish." (John 1: 1-4)*

The prophet Isaiah implored us be "a light unto the nations"; to be active participants in shaping the world around us.

The Sovereign God of Israel says;

> *"Forget what happened (to you) in the past. Do not dwell on the events of long ago. (For) I AM going to do a new thing. It's already happened. Do you not recognize (perceive) it?" (Isaiah 43: 18-19)*

As Jesus said to the Samaritan woman at "Jacob's Well";

> *"For (by receiving) the water I give, you'll never thirst again. The water I give will become an effervescent spring, bubbling up within you." (John 4: 11-14)*

Jesus was described as "the Word", the embodiment of the essence of God Most High.

Given that the LORD God declared humankind into existence by virtue of the Word, we, being "made in God's image", are imprinted with a type of "signature" of our Maker.

Does that mean "God-within-us" at core level; such as a sense of "eternity" inscribed (embedded) on the double-helix spiral structure known as human "DNA?" Probably!

No matter how deeply buried or dormant, the imprint of God, the Creator was or still is, the Holy Spirit reinvigorates, revitalizes and rejuvenates the signature of God, within.

The name Adam derives from the Hebrew word, "adamah", meaning, earth, ground, or clay. Thankfully, God, the Master Potter, determined that we men and women, "formed of dust" needed a bit of "watering", to moisten our dry, hardened, brittle "vessels", making you and I more malleable.

> *"The first man (Adam) became a living-being (having been animated by the breath of life); but the 'Second Adam' (Yeshua) is life-giving spirit." (1 Corinthians 15: 45)*

The Inaugural First Couple's decision to partake from the Tree deemed "off-limits" caused a "divine-dilemma" of sorts. For how could the high-voltage holiness (intensity) God's glory further occupy the same "sacred" space (in Eden) as the compromised psyche of Man? What would it take to cover the experience of "nakedness" (exposure)? What would God do to remedy the symptomology associated with Original Sin (feelings of guilt and shame which weren't even part of Man's emotional repertoire, previously?

> *"All is from God, who through Christ, reconciled us to Himself. And He has given to us the ministry of reconciliation." (2 Corinthians 5: 18-19)*

The Good News

From the beginning, God, the Creator, intended to dwell with creation. Unfortunately, the debacle in Eden left Adam and Eve experiencing "nakedness", which is to say, the removal

3

of God's covering. Per divine-design, we, the descendants of Adam, cannot cover "nakedness" with a fig-leaf fashion-statement. Sure, it would be nice, if we, the descendants of Adam and Eve, could simply put forbidden-fruit back on the tree, and/or erase, undo, or purge-away the introduction of doubt (sin) into the human psyche. Fortunately, what we could not accomplish in and of ourselves, the LORD our God did on our behalf.

The Holy One of Israel says;

> *"I am the One who blots out your sins for My own sake; I will remember them no more." (Isaiah 43: 25)*

The crimson-chord running through Scripture culminated at the Cross, whereby God's judgment and His mercy were fused into One.

> *"Now, 'in Christ', you who were once distant, are brought near. The partition (dividing-wall, enmity), which is to say, separation from God which characterized the human condition is no more, by virtue of the blood which was shed on the Cross For He is our peace; creating in Himself, one new man in place of the two (double-mindedness); thus, establishing peace." (Ephesians 2: 13-15)*

Jesus, the "anomaly with anointing", absorbed the divine-penalty, which in effect, gave God cause to mark the sin-debt incurred through Adam, "paid in full."

*"In Him, we have redemption; the forgiveness
of sins according to the richness of His grace."
(Ephesians 1: 7)*

*The Heavenly Father (by way of the Son) draws us back
into covenantal relationship by re-igniting the "flame of
remembrance" inscribed/instilled within us.*

The Mystery

We don't need to understand the mystery to know God exists.

*Human nature is prone to project its' self-limiting (self-
disqualifying) ego-centric thoughts onto the infinite, multi-
faceted Creator, who is, was, and forever-will-be."*

*Moses expressed doubt about what he'd heard from the voice
of God; prompting, what could be described as a teachable
moment, for us all.*

> *"Who is it who make mouths for men to talk,
> who makes ears for men to hear, or makes them
> deaf or speechless, clear-sighted or blind? It is I,
> the LORD (the Eternal, Jehovah, the Creator).
> So, go, and I will be with you, instructing
> (teaching) you what to say." (Exodus 4: 10-12)*

The LORD instructed Moses;

> *"Speak to Aaron and his sons (the origins of the
> priesthood), instructing them, 'This is the way*

you shall bless the children of Israel: Say, 'The LORD bless you and keep you! The LORD let His face shine upon you. May He be gracious to you. May God lift His countenance to you (look upon you kindly); and give you peace'."
(Numbers 6: 23-26)

It isn't a stretch to say the key to understanding the connection between the Aaronic-blessing, and "new-covenant" blessings, is the Holy Name.

"So, shall they (the Levites, serving as priests) put My Name on the children of Israel, and I (the LORD) will bless them." (Numbers 6: 27)

In communing with God the Father, Jesus the Son, said, "This is eternal life; to know You, the only true God; and (to know) Jesus, the Christ, whom you sent." (John 17: 3)

"I made Your name known to those who You gave me (from this world)." (John 17: 6)

"While I was with them, I kept them safe by the power of Your Name; the name you gave me." (John 17: 12)

Moses told God, "please, LORD, I am not a good speaker. I've never been a good speaker, and I am not a good speaker now (even after You, speaking with me). I become tongue-tied, easily." In response to Moses' self-assessment, God, the Creator of the Man, rhetorically asked Moses;

"Who is it who make mouths for men to talk, who makes ears for men to hear, or makes them deaf or speechless, clear-sighted or blind? It is I, the LORD (the Eternal, Jehovah, the Creator). So, go, and I will be with you, instructing (teaching) you what to say." (Exodus 4: 10-12)

Lost in Translation

Scripture records;

> *"At one time the whole earth had one language; and people used the same words (spoke a single language)." (Genesis 11: 1)*

From Scripture we learn the LORD God (Elohim) didn't approve of the construction-project known as the Tower of Babel.

The descendants of Noah's three sons had migrated to the plains of Babylonia (the land of Shinar), where they determined it was a good idea to build a city, replete with a monumental tower, honoring themselves.

> *"Come, let's us build ourselves a city, having a tower with a top stretching into the heavens; a monument to our greatness (let us make a name for ourselves). This will bring us together; lest we be scattered over the face of the earth." (Genesis 11: 3–4)*

7

According to Scripture, "the LORD came down (descended) to see the city, and the tower, that Adam's descendants were building." (Genesis 11: 5)

Apparently, the ziggurat-style structure (possibly a rudimentary observatory intended for "star-gazing"), the LORD God (Elohim) determined that the course of mankind was in need of "an intervention."

> *"The proposed building-program was terminated. And God scattered the people over the face of the earth. The LORD confounded them, giving the people different languages so they would not understand one another's speech." (Genesis 11: 7-8)*

The LORD reiterated the point in noting the absurdity of clay dictating to the Potter, what it shall become. The same theme is expressed in the Book of Job, where the LORD God chided Job for "jumping to the wrong conclusion" based on limited understanding.

> *"Can you bind the cluster of the Pleiades? Or loose the bel of Orion? Can bring out the Mazzaroth in its season? Can you guide the Great Bear with its cubs? Do you know the ordinances of the heavens?" (Job 38: 31-33)*

Before the LORD restored Job's fortunes, the righteous servant (Job) issued an "admission of ignorance"; saying,

"I heard of You before, but now that I have seen You with my own eyes, I take back (retract) what I said (in my ignorance)." (Job 42: 5-6)

According to Scripture, dissonance (misunderstanding) is pretty much "a given."

"Ever since the creation of the universe, the invisible qualities of God (the Creator) have been clearly seen; made understandable from what he has made. People know who God is, yet they do not glorify Him, nor do they offer Him praise." (Romans 1: 20-21)

At Babel, God, the Creator, scrambled (distorted) the "channels of communication." Yet, most wondrously, the LORD God untangled "the language-barrier", which He, Himself, had imposed.

"The name given the city (the location where this occurred) was called 'Babel', because it was there God confused (confounded) the speech of the world." (Genesis 11: 9)

Given the location of the "cradle of civilization" (and the Garden of Eden), it is reasonable to think the "pre-babble" idiom of humankind was the Semitic-tongue of Hebrew. And in that light, there's every reason to believe that the dispensation of the Holy Spirit is divinely purposed to "bridge" the language-barrier between peoples and nations.

From Scripture we learn that, early on, humankind went astray to the point, "They exchanged the glorious truth of God, for the lie; becoming enamored with ("worshiped") created things, instead of the Creator; the One holding the power of creation.

In other words;

Note: The Abrahamic promise stands in sharp contrast to human nature's skewed propensity to tout or brand itself, to "go it alone", at God's expense.

The LORD told Abram;

> *"I will make you a great nation. I will bless you. And I will make your name great; you will be a blessing. And I will bless those who bless you." (Genesis 12: 2-3)*

The Testimony

I was a guest at a holistic health retreat, and I volunteered to work a few hours a day at the facility. As God, or fate, would have it, I was beginning my stay, as another volunteer was finishing theirs'. The timing was perfect, because it meant taking over the job of the departing guest, who had been responsible for watering the plants and edible scrubs of the garden. The man asked me if I'd be willing to help him write a testimonial about the progress he'd made while at the health retreat. He told me: "My name is Joseph. I am Israeli. In my younger days, I was a competitive bodybuilder. In fact, I won the title of 'Mr. Israel' in the mid 70's (1970's)." As impressive as all of this sounded, what he said next really caught my attention. He said, "I am extremely sun-sensitive."

I tried to not let my facial expression betray my curiosity and surprise. For, I too, had suffered with bouts of sun-sensitivity. So, I figured in assisting Joseph with his testimony, I might gain insight into my own history (and possibly, destiny).

I recently traveled to Israel, prompted by the belief that God had something in store for me. Shortly after arriving, I was forced to hunker down in my hotel lobby, because snow from a chilling winter storm was tying up transportation. A woman approached me, and she pointed to the book that was perched up against my laptop. Astonishingly, her husband was the book's "writer." She asked me if I'd like to meet him. I nodded, "yes", not really expecting David H. Stern, the translator of THE JEWISH NEW TESTAMENT, to walk out of the elevator. He explained the rare set of circumstances that had led him to be at the hotel. Transit into and out of Jerusalem (the place he and his wife call home) was blocked-off because of the snow; and he was just waiting for the road to re-open. Biblically-speaking, I can certainly relate to being relegated to a "holding-pattern."

I mean, only an hour earlier, I'd been bemoaning the inclement weather for disrupting my sight-seeing itinerary. But now I was, praising God; for the stormy conditions had put me in position to receive the confirmation I was seeking (in Israel).

Yes, I have overcome the spiritual malady of Son (of Man) sensitivity.

Words Matter

The blessings spoken over brothers Judah and Joseph by the family patriarch Jacob, are like instrumental-keys sounding pitch-perfect notes in God's grand symphony. Biblically-speaking, Yeshua, the Messiah, represents a spirit-infused "amalgamation" of the blessings and attributes of sons Judah and of Joseph. The salvation plan restores the all-important link between the tribe of Joseph and the tribe of Judah.

> *"Judah, your brothers will praise you. You will defeat your enemies. Your father's sons will bow before you. The scepter will not depart from Judah, nor the ruler's staff from between his feet until the coming of the One to whom it belongs; the one whom nations will obey. He will tie his donkey to a grapevine, and (tether) his colt to a choice vine. He washes his clothes in wine because his harvest is so plentiful." (Genesis 49: 8-11)*

> *"Joseph is a fruitful tree; a fruitful tree besides a fountain. He has been attacked by archers, who shot and harassed him. But his bow remained strong, and his arms were strengthened by the Mighty One of Jacob, the Shepherd, and Rock of Israel. May the God of your ancestors help you; the Almighty bless you with blessings of the heavens above, blessings of the earth beneath, and blessings of the breasts (sustenance), and of the womb (fruitfulness)." (Genesis 49: 22-26)*

And if the spoken blessing weren't enough, the names given the two brothers by their respective mothers (Leah of Judah and Rachel of Joseph) convey the overriding theme God's story of redemption and restoration; whereby "praising God" and the "removal of shame" are integrally linked.

> *"Leah became pregnant again. She gave birth to another son; (but) this time I will praise the LORD. She named him Judah, meaning, 'praise.'" (Genesis 29: 35)*

And the LORD remembered Rachel;

> *"God answered her prayers. She became pregnant, and gave birth to a son; saying, 'God has removed (taken away) my shame (disgrace)." (Genesis 30: 23)*

In recalling divine principles, the "sprinkling of blood on the doorposts and doorframes of Israelite houses, effectively "demarcated" those dwelling places for safe-keeping. In a similar, and yet, altogether different way, Jesus, as both "the Door", and the Lamb, takes the Feast of Passover to another level.

Biblically-speaking, "rolling away of the stone" in order that the sheep could be watered, serves as a glimpse of the resurrection power of the LORD God, who on the "third day" blew the lid off the tomb's covering so the entire flock could receive the spirit of life eternal. Recall, "when Jacob approached a well so his flocks could receive water, he saw three flocks of sheep lying down, lined-up, waiting to be watered. Jacob asked the local herdsmen about what was

going on, and the local herdsmen explained that customarily, they'd wait until all the flocks were present, before rolling the stone off the mouth of the well. While Jacob was still talking with them, a shepherdess arrived with her father's sheep. And upon learning the woman was the daughter of his uncle Laban, Jacob stepped forward and he proceeded to "roll away the stone."
(Genesis 29: 2–11)

May Rachel's tears for her children's children be forever comforted.

> *"Now the Lord says, "Do not weep any longer, for I will reward you. Your children will come back to you from distant lands; and there is hope for your future." (Jeremiah 31: 16-17)*

Branches, Trees, and Nations

Some have speculated early Hebrew scribes debated the wisdom (or efficacy) of placing the Word of God on the printed page (papyrus scrolls). They were probably concerned whether the awesome power of God...the Eternal could be adequately conveyed "bound to text?" As it turned out, their writings became the "basis of religion."

Biblically speaking, the word "tree" often served as a metaphor in describing "nations."

After triumphing over the Midianites, the people were exhorting Gideon to take the role of ruling leader (king-like figure) of Israel. But to his credit, Gideon's wisdom quieted the people's errant assumptions. Gideon simply stated, "the LORD will rule over you!" (Judges 8: 23)

Not long after Gideon's death, a half-brother of "Gideon's seventy sons" attempted to usurp the throne (become king). He tried coercing the people of Shechem to get behind his crooked agenda, coyly asking them if they'd prefer to be "governed" by all seventy of Gideon's sons, or, ruled over by one man. Apparently, their response didn't matter, because he had all seventy of his half-brothers killed—or so he thought.

Jotham, the youngest son of Gideon, escaped. His was the "voice of reason" for those who could see "the forest through the trees."

> *"Listen to me, citizens of Shechem, if you want God to listen to you! Once upon a time the trees decided to elect a king. So they said to the olive tree, 'Be our king!' But the olive tree refused, saying, 'Should I quit producing the olive oil that blesses both God and people in order to wave back and forth over the trees?' Then they (the trees) said to the fig tree, 'Be our king!' But the fig tree refused, saying, 'Should I quit producing sweet fruit, just to wave back and forth over the trees?' Then they said to the grapevine, 'Be our king!' But the grapevine refused, saying, 'Should I quit producing wine, which cheers both God and people, to wave back and forth over the trees?' Then they*

turned to the thorn-bush, and said, 'Be our king!' And the thorn-bush said, "If you want to make me king take shelter under my shade; but if not, let fire come from me, and devour the cedars of Lebanon." (Judges 9: 7–15)

Jotham's parable provided a glimpse of what was to come in the form of a sobering-prediction issued by the LORD God, Himself.

Samuel, the last of the Judges of Israel (Gideon preceded Samuel) warned the Israelites about the "less than ideal" attributes they could expect from an earthly king. Yet the people refused to heed Samuel's wise counsel.

The LORD God consoled Samuel, and told him;

"Listen to what the people say; they are not rejecting you; (rather) they are rejecting Me as their King." (1 Samuel 8: 6-7)

Is not the euphemism, "Be careful what you ask, because you just might get it", apropos for this day and age? The Israelites had insisted they'd be better off with a militaristic-type leader, of the sort "ruling the other nations." As God, the Creator, has been known to do, He "stepped aside" as to allow "the will of the people to rule." Problem is: Human nature is prone to make non-redemptive choices, leading to futility. From that perspective, human nature getting what it insists on having is "a penance", of sorts.

An interesting aside relating to the "Jewish-experience" in America, is shortly after Rhode Island ratified the Constitution to join the newly formed republic of the United States, George Washington visited the city of Newport (in Rhode Island) to gain support for what is now known as "The Bill of Rights." The welcoming committee that greeted the President included a man named Moses Mendes Seixas, the head of the Touro Synagogue, a congregation founded in the mid-1600's by Jewish families of Spanish and Portuguese descent that made their way to the New World by way of Brazil and Barbados. The Rabbi used the opportunity (the President's visit) to address the issue of religious liberty (freedom to worship), and the "separation of church (temple) and state." Interestingly, in those days, speaking about the "division of church and state", meant voicing people's concerns about governing institutions infringing on the rights of the faithful. In other words, the Founding Fathers were out to protect Judeo-Christion principles. Today, the reverse is true. George Washington and Moses Seixas both championed the cause of freedom, faith, and religious tolerance.

The name of the congregation headed by Rabbi Moses Seixas was Yeshuat Israel; the name alone speaks to the LORD's mission statement.

> *"An angel of the Lord appeared to Joseph, and told him, 'Joseph, son of David, do not be afraid to take Mary into your home as your wife, for the child within her was conceived by the Holy Spirit. She will bear a son, and you are to name him*

'Yeshua', meaning, Yah (God) saves. He will save his people from their sins.'" (Matthew 1: 20-21)

Book of Grace

If only we could climb the rungs of "Jacob's Ladder", and ascend step by step above the maze-like machinations of the world, surely then, from a vantage point on High, a new-found clarity would reveal the Book of Law was purposed to magnify (highlight) man's fallen nature, necessitating the Book of Grace.

> *"Because of the blood of Your covenant, I the LORD, will set your prisoners free from the waterless pit (dry well). Return to your stronghold, you prisoners of hope. For even now (at this late date), I will restore double to you." (Zechariah 9: 11-12)*

The Word Ladder

Jacob set his head on a "stone–pillow", and he dosed off.

> *"He dreamt of a stairway ('ladder') that rested on the ground, with its top reaching up to the heavens. On it, he saw the angels of God, going up (ascending) and descending." (Genesis 28: 11-12)*

And there was the LORD above the top rung, saying;

*"I AM the Lord, the God of Abraham, and your
father Isaac. In you, and your descendants, all
the families of the earth will find blessing. I AM
with you. I will bring you back to this land. I will
not leave you, until I (the Lord) have done all
that I promised." (Genesis 28: 14–15)*

Now, fast forward to the arrival of the Messiah.

*"Philip, who was from Bethsaida (the same
town as Andrew and Peter) found Nathaniel,
and enthusiastically to him; 'We've found the
One about whom Moses wrote, whom the
prophets spoke of, the Messiah, Yeshua, the
son of Joseph." (John 1: 45)*

Nathaniel's dismissive response illustrates just how
presumptuous human nature can be; quick to jump to the
wrong conclusion based limited understanding.

*"Can anything good come from Nazareth?"
(John 1: 46)*

He errantly assumed that "nothing of value" could come from
the sleepy "backwards" village of Nazareth.

Philip was undaunted; telling Nathaniel to "come and see!"

Yeshua later explained;

*"You shall see even greater things than this.
You will see the sky (the heavens) opened, and*

> the angels of God going up (ascending) and descending on the Son of Man." (John 1: 50-51)

A person's willingness to believe (faith) activates God's faithfulness to promises.

The miracle of Israel is a testament to the restorative power of God...Eternal. And the Messiah's story is a reconstituted version of "Jacob's (Israel's) journey."

> "You are My witnesses. I have chosen you as My servant, so that you can know Me. I AM the LORD." (Isaiah 43: 10)

Those with eyes of faith witness "Jacob's ladder", personified.

Spirit of Emmanuel

The sixth chapter of Isaiah has been referred to as "the Book of Emmanuel." Isaiah's sentiments echo the challenge of "walking in faith, and not by sight."

If there were such a thing as "divine-sarcasm", the following verses surely qualify.

> "I heard the voice of the LORD, saying, 'Whom shall I send? Who will go?' And I answered, 'Here I am Lord, send me.' And the LORD responded, telling me, 'Go, and say to this people; 'Listen and listen, but never understand! Look and look, but never perceive! Yes, make this people's

heart hard, make their ears dull, and shut their eyes, lest they use their eyes to see, use their ears to hear, use their hearts to understand, and thus be changed, and be healed." (Isaiah 6: 8-10)

That's a paradox, rolled into a conundrum.

In the Book of Isaiah, we're alerted to the challenges that a person of faith can expect day to day, amidst surrounding doubt and skepticism.

"I (Isaiah) saw the LORD sitting on a high throne. There were angels with six wings standing above Him; with two of the wings they covered their faces, with two of the wings they covered their feet, and with two they flew. And they called to each other; saying, 'Holy, holy, holy is the LORD of Armies! The whole earth is filled with His glory.' Their voices shook the foundations of the doorposts of the Temple. And I (Isaiah) said to myself, 'I am doomed! Every word that passes through my lips is unclean (relative to the holiness of God). I live among people with unclean (sinful) lips. I have seen the King, the LORD of Armies! Then one of the angels flew over to me and touched my lips with a burning coal taken with tongs from the holy altar. He (the angel) touched my mouth with it; saying, 'This (coal) has touched your lips. Your guilt has been taken away

(removed). And your sins have been forgiven."
(Isaiah 6: 1-7)

So, if you happen to be feeling inadequate, and pretty much "wretched" relative to the holiness of Adonai (God), know that you're in good company. The LORD's mouthpiece, the prophet Isaiah, needed the touch from a "cleansing-agent", before he had what it took to deliver the message with power and authority.

We are not at liberty to dismiss the divine symmetry in Isaiah, the prophet's name; "Isaiah" aptly translates, "the LORD will save."

> *"The Lord, Himself, will give you this sign: A virgin will conceive, and give birth to a son. And she will call him, 'Emmanuel', meaning, 'God-with-us')." (Isaiah 7: 14)*

> *"For a child is born to us, a son is given; and upon his shoulder dominion rests. He will be named, Wonderful-Counselor, Everlasting-Father, and the Prince of Peace." (Isaiah 9: 5)*

The few times that the angel Gabriel is mentioned in the Bible, heralded a "news-flash" of yes, biblical proportion (as in the Book of Enoch, the Book of Daniel, and in the New Testament). So, for Gabriel to show up in the town of Nazareth, as if right on cue per the Book of Daniel, equates to a page-turning, calendar-changing event.

The Divine Equation

> *"Faith (trusting God) is the confidence of what we hope for shall come to pass; convinced about things not yet seen. By faith we understand that the entire universe was formed (originated) by the spoken (declared) Word of God." (Hebrews 11: 1-3)*

God is Spirit; and Spirit is not beholden to a world that revolves around numbers ($$$). Do not despair when things seemingly "don't add up", For the Spirit of God, in you, is a life-changing revelation that transcends the so-called, "natural order of things."

So, if you happen to be feeling overwhelmed, as if you're caught in the riptide-like undertow of society at large, know the Spirit of the LORD is a giant life-preserver.

> *"As the waters (of the Flood) increased, the ark was lifted; and it rose above the earth. The waters prevailed, and the ark glided about on the surface of the waters." (Genesis 7: 17-18)*

Ride the wave of spirit-infused revelation.

The ways of God are anomalous to our way of thinking.

Recall, the inhabitants of Jericho approached Elisha (Elijah's successor), saying;

"The location of this city is fine, but the water is bad." Elisha instructed them to bring him a new jar, and to put some salt in it." Scripture says that Elisha went to the spring, and he proceeded to toss salt into the foul-tasting water; announcing, "This is what the LORD says, 'I have healed (purified) this water. No more death or barrenness (infertility) will come from it." (2 Kings 2: 19-21)

The Ruach-HaKodesh (the Holy Spirit) is not solely "a New Testament thing."

Scripture records numerous instances in which the LORD our God "poured out His Spirit."

When Moses summoned seventy leaders of Israel to come to the Tabernacle.

The LORD to him;

"I will take some of the Spirit that is on you, and I will put the Spirit upon them, also. They will bear the burden of the people, so you won't have to carry it alone." (Numbers 11: 16–17)

The Spirit of the LORD is an "equal opportunity" employer.

"She (Wisdom) is a tree of life to those who take firm hold of her; those who cling to her (wisdom) are blessed. By wisdom the LORD laid the foundation of the earth." (Proverbs 3: 18-19)

"My son, do not lose sight of this: priceless is wisdom, and foresight; they will be life to you."
(Proverbs 21-22)

The Holy Spirit has been poured out (dispensed) so that we might connect the biblical dots ushering us back to God's refuge.

"I (the LORD) will pour My Spirit on everyone. Your sons and daughters will prophesy, your old men will dream dreams, and your young men will see visions. In those days, I (the LORD) will pour My Spirit on the servants, on both men and women. I shall work miracles in the sky, and on the earth; blood, fire, and clouds of smoke. The sun will darken, and the moon will become as red as blood (the "blood moon"), before the Great and Dreadful Day of the LORD arrives." (Joel 2: 28-29)

In the Old Testament, the element of water was often used to symbolize the Spirit. So, in times of turmoil and dissension, when the gridlock at ground level is off the charts, keep your eyes of faith affixed on God's promises.

The Holy Spirit comforts us by "unveiling" God's overriding plan.

We are directed to the Word instilled within.

"You belong to God (imprinted with His signature). You have won the victory; for

greater is the One who is in you, than he who is in the world." (1 John 4)

"And do not call conspiracy everything this people calls 'a conspiracy.' Do not fear what they fear; do not dread it." (Isaiah 8: 12)

Fire Born of Water

The seeds of salvation were planted from the beginning.

"The first man (Adam) became a living-being (animated by the breath of life). Whereas, Christ Jesus, a type of 'Second Adam', is life-giving spirit." (1 Corinthians 15: 45)

The carbon-laden dust from which Man was formed is subject to gravity. Nevertheless, the "fallen vessel" is uplifted by the Spirit of God.

"The Helper (or, Comforter), namely, the Holy Spirit, whom the Father will send in My name (advocating on behalf of Messiah), will teach you all things. The Holy Spirit will bring to your remembrance all the things I said (taught) you." (John 14: 26)

The Holy Spirit advocates for Truth.

"When He, the Spirit of Truth, comes, He will guide you into all Truth; for He will not speak *on His own authority, but He shall speak what He hears (from the Father), and tell you of things to come." (John 16: 13)*

The Holy Spirit raises people's awareness. And there comes a point when grace-consciousness surpasses sin-consciousness a believer's psyche.

> *"You have been delivered by grace; and even this was not your accomplishment; it's God's freely-given gift. And 'in Christ', you're created a-new, so you may do all the things God already planned." (Ephesians 2: 8-10)*

> *"When a person turns to the LORD, the veil (partition) is removed. God is Spirit; and where the spirit of the LORD is, there is freedom." (2 Corinthians 3: 16-17)*

The Kingdom of God (which is rooted in Spirit) and the "ways of the world" grate on each other, and the interaction between the two creates something "anew." As a grain of sand inside an oyster serves as a catalyst-like "irritant" for pearl production, so does the Spirit of the LORD interact with our spirit inside… out; transforming us into walking-talking "pearls of wisdom."

It's as if one's willingness to believe (faith) determines God's provision; and like "manna from heaven", wisdom is distributed incrementally, bit by bit.

The ways of God are anomalous to our way of thinking.

Recall, the inhabitants of Jericho approached Elisha (Elijah's successor), saying;

> *"The location of this city is fine, but the water is bad." Elisha instructed them to bring him a new jar, and to put some salt in it." Scripture says that Elisha went to the spring, and he proceeded to toss salt into the foul-tasting water; announcing, "This is what the LORD says, 'I have healed (purified) this water. No more death or barrenness (infertility) will come from it." (2 Kings 2: 19-21)*

To be born (reborn) of water (signifying, Spirit) is to grasp the gist of what Jesus was saying to the disciples.

> *"No one puts new wine into old wineskins; (for) if he does, the new wine will burst the skins, spill out, and the skins, too, will be ruined. On the contrary, new wine must be put into freshly prepared wineskins." (Luke 5: 37-38)*

The Ripple-Effect

In reflecting on the story of David and Goliath, it wasn't a stone, per se, that felled the Philistine giant, but rather the gemstone-like trust that David placed in God.

> *"You (Goliath) come to me with sword, spear, and javelin, but I come to you in the name of the Lord— God of Heaven's armies—the God*

of Israel. Everyone assembled here will know that the Lord rescues His people; this is the Lord's battle." (1 Samuel 17: 45-46)

David, the seventh son of Jesse, unified the divided Kingdom of Israel by bringing the Ark of the LORD's Covenant to a town having a perennial water supply. There, at a junction of roadways, David set the Ark on "higher ground" (Jerusalem).

Have you ever expected someone else to take initiative, but they show no inclination to do so? And then you get irritated, because they don't seem see (understand) what's obvious to you. Maybe God places blinders over people's eyes, as to prevent divine-truths from being revealed, prematurely (before a spirit-based foundation has been a person has been to integrate, or fully appreciate.

Many picture David as a man whose star was constantly on the rise; actually, his life was filled with many peaks and valleys. He was oppressed, vilified, cast out, and forced to wait more than a decade for his royal appointment to materialize.

Who among David's friends would have blamed him, if he just aborted the mission? But for David, stopping short of the destination would be equivalent to sabotaging his own destiny.

David's patience paid off when the LORD God cleared the path to the throne.

A Sling and a Stone

It's not about man's "call to arms", nor is it about winning through overwhelming fire power, vanquishing an opponent by brute force, or carnal might.

Victory is at hand by rallying for the LORD; and blessing what God blesses.

As the shepherd boy David so eloquently noted;

> *"You (Goliath) come to me with sword and spear; but I come to you in the Name of the LORD, God of the Armies of Israel. Those assemble here shall know (learn) that it's not by sword or spear that the LORD saves. It is the LORD's battle (to win), and He will deliver." (1 Samuel 17: 45-47)*

How important is the presence of the LORD (the Spirit) in shaping a person's life?

King David put it this way:

> *"LORD, renew a faithful spirit in me. Do not take (remove) Your Holy Spirit away from me. Restore to me the joy of your salvation ('Yeshua'); uphold me by Your merciful Spirit." (Psalms 51: 10-11)*

> *"The LORD is compassionate, merciful, patient, and always ready to forgive. He has*

not treated us we deserve (as our wrong-doing warrants)." (Psalms 103: 8-10)

The Legacy

I turned on my lap-top this morning to read a critique of a question posed by boxing champ Manny Pacquiao to the Miss Universe contestant representing the U.S.A. Just a few days before, I'd been on a flight from Manila to Los Angeles, and a couple of rows in front, sat the Eight-Division World Champion (without an entourage). I figured he was venturing from the Philippines to sign the contract for the most highly anticipated match of his career against the undefeated Floyd Mayweather. But that wasn't the case. He was headed to Doral, Florida to guest on the panel of judges for the 2015 Miss Universe contest.

As part of the competition, Manny's guest appearance on the telecast entailed posing a question that delved into more than just the physical attributes of pageant contestants. Miss U.S.A. drew Mr. Pacquiao as the one who'd ask her a question. "If you had 30 seconds to deliver a message to a global terrorist, what would you say?"

Apparently, some of the viewing public were bothered by the "saccharine-sweet" answer offered by Miss U.S.A., who suggested that a message of peace and love might quell the actions of terrorists. While other viewers were upset that Mr. Pacquiao dared to ask such a thought-provoking question in the context of a beauty-competition.

Note: How things have changed in America since 2015. Now, the phrase "domestic-terrorism" is a prime topic of conversation.

The trajectory of Emmanuel "Manny" Pacquiao's career has progressed in stages. From a rail-thin featherweight to his David versus Goliath-like conquests over fighters far bigger than he, has given fans good reason to say, Emmanuel D. Pacquiao, "God-is-with-you."

In the context of combat-sports, fighters strive to dominate their opponent with tenacious bravado. That's why seeing Manny gesture to a referee to step-in, and mercifully stop a bout so his badly beaten opponent would be spared any further damage, was exasperating, yet fitting, to see. Emmanuel Pacquiao's understands the power of mercy.

As is his custom, Emmanuel D. Pacquiao kneels in his corner before the opening-bell, offering prayers for both himself, and his opponent.

The pundits of pugilism failed to recognize that Emmanuel's (Manny's) ascent up the ranks has shown signs of God's hand.

> *"Not by might, and not by carnal strength (will you prevail); but by My Spirit, says the Lord of Hosts." (Zechariah 4: 6)*

Talk about the "one-two punch" of a champion:

"The Lord who created and formed you says;
'Do not fear, for I have redeemed you and
called you by name." (Isaiah 43: 1-2)

"I (the Lord) have called you back from the ends
of the earth so you can serve. Do not be afraid;
I AM with you. Do not be dismayed; for I AM
the LORD; I will uphold you with my victorious
right hand." (Isaiah 41: 9-10)

To be "called by name" is not so much about the given-name
on your Birth Certificate, but rather the name of the God-
appointed One, calling you and I, in the "name of salvation."

"You (a person of faith) belong to God; and
thus, you have overcome. You have won the
victory, because He who is in you (the Spirit
of the LORD) is greater than he who is in the
world." (1 John 4; 4)

"By His mighty power at work in us, we are
well-able to accomplish more than we ever
thought possible." (Ephesians 3: 20)

All of us face daunting odds in one way or another; it's part
of the human-condition. And maybe like Gideon of the Old
Testament, you, too, have felt like crying out to God. "O' Lord,
how can I possibly deliver (accomplish the divinely-assigned
task or mission) Israel, when my family is the poorest in the
territory of Manasseh (one of Joseph's sons)." (Judges 6: 15)

I am sure there were times when Manny Pacquiao felt like the "fate of the entire nation" was riding on his diminutive shoulders. Yet, like the message communicated to Gideon, those "in Christ" are equipped, spiritually, for God's victory, achieved through the blood of the Lamb.

> *"The Lord is with you. Go with the strength you have." (Judges 6: 12)*

The theatrical-adage, "the show must go on", aptly described the Mayweather-Pacquiao extravaganza; for on that night, Manny's usual good-natured upbeat appearance happened to be masking concern about a shoulder injury (actually, a torn rotator-cuff) suffered in the days leading up to the big-fight. But "Manny being Manny" did not want to disappoint the world-wide viewing audience, and thus, he climbed into the ring that night, in what most of us think of as "a classic no-win" situation.

Yet despite the hype and hoopla, Emmanuel Pacquiao has maintained the heart of a servant. Whether he's working up a sweat in the gym, or he's entering the stage ("lion's den") of the MGM Grand Arena, the words printed on his white T-shirt, inform spectators where his heart is: "Jesus is the Name of the Lord."

From the early days in General Santos City, when "lacing up the gloves" meant wrapping crudely-patched together fabric around his fists to his multi-million dollar prize-fights, the kid, who'd been forced by impoverished circumstances to cast his nets into the sea in order to have food to eat, now, has come to epitomize what Jesus meant in saying to Simon and Andrew, *"Follow me! I will teach you how to be fishers of men." (Mark 1: 17)*

Post-script:

The Championship Fight was decided by the judges' scorecards. Even if one's fellow man (human judges) do not recognize, or reward, a person's willingness to journey far from home, and go to battle in the opponent's hometown (Las Vegas), we believe that the God in Heaven rewards, and in fact, has already rewarded your trust in Him. According to the judges at ringside, Manny's opponent won the fight; but in no way should that be interpreted to mean he, a person of faith, lost the war. In fact, "the rematch" played out in the Federal Court of Las Vegas, with plaintiffs (certain paid ticket holders) contending they've been defrauded, because the fight didn't live up to the plaintiff's expectations.

In sports, maintaining the "competitive advantage", means that athletes do not telegraph the report of a weakened area of their anatomy to the opponent to target and exploit.

The legal case against Emmanuel "Pacman" Pacquiao was dropped.

But as people of faith well know, the resistance and opposition still present a challenge.

Some questioned whether "Pacman" (Pacquiao) had become "too religious" for the merciless sport of boxing. But what the naysayers fail to realize is that all the descendants of Adam and Eve are in the fray, so to speak, on a "spiritual-battlefield." For that reason, we familiarize ourselves with the spirit-based weaponry that the LORD supplies.

> *"They (the brethren 'in Christ') have won the victory by virtue of the blood of the Lamb, and the word of their testimony." (Revelation 12: 11)*

Note: How serendipitous that the winner of the 2018 Miss Universe Contest was a Filipina (born in Queensland, Australia)?

As Esther, a former beauty-pageant winner, and the one-time Queen of Persia, might advise, "Looks can open a few doors", but for the doors to stay open, humbly give credit where credit is due.

May you be like "an Esther", in your generation, "for such a time as this."

The Suffering Servant

The prophets of Israel took no pleasure in delivering harsh words to God's people; but a prophet's "calling" superseded personal preferences, biases, comfort-level and convenience.

> *"Because I love Israel, and because my heart yearns for Jerusalem, I cannot remain silent. I will not stop praying until her righteousness shines like the dawn; her salvation blazes like a burning torch." (Isaiah 62: 1)*

Isaiah implored us be "a light unto the nations"; in other words, "active-participants" in shaping the world around us.

> *"You are my servant (Israel); and you shall bring Me (the LORD) glory. The One commissioning me to bring His people back to Him, says, 'You will do more than just restore the people of Israel, I will make you a light to the nations, and you'll bring My salvation to the ends of the earth'." (Isaiah 49: 5-6)*

Whether one thinks of Israel as "the suffering servant", or Jesus of Nazareth as the "righteous (and suffering) servant", their stories are irrevocably linked.

Between the LORD's vineyard, Israel, and Jesus, "the vine", the God of Israel provides shelter for all.

> *"There was nothing beautiful or majestic about his appearance; nothing of physical stature to attract (or garner) a following. He was despised and rejected—a man of sorrows, who was acquainted with the bitterest grief. Yet it was our weaknesses (frailties) that he carried; it was our sorrows that weighed him down. We thought his troubles were a punishment from God; instead, he was wounded and crushed for our transgressions. He was beaten (scourged) so we might have peace. By his stripes (his wounds) we are healed." (Isaiah 53: 2-7)*

"When his life is made an offering (for sin), he will have a multitude of children, and many heirs (to God's promises). For on account of what his sacrifice (absorbing the divine penalty under the Law), he made it possible for many to be counted as righteous. And I (the LORD) will give him the honor (and glory) of one who is mighty. (For) he bore the sins of many, interceding for sinners." (Isaiah 53: 10-12)

It's always timely to revisit the Book of Daniel.

The way is revealed like a "trail of bread-crumbs."

"Those who endure will be saved. The good news about the Kingdom will be preached throughout the world. The time will come when you'll see what Daniel, the prophet, spoke about; pay close attention!" (Matthew 24: 13-15)

The God of Heaven is recorded to have done the miraculous during the reign of king Nebuchadnezzar. Scripture says, the three Judean captives, Hananiah, Mishael, and Azariah (whose Babylonian names were Shadrach, Meshach, and Abednego) were thrown into the white-hot flames of a furnace. "So huge were the flames, the Babylonian soldiers who'd thrown the three into the white-hot fire, were themselves devoured by the blazing flames." (Daniel 3: 22)

King Nebuchadnezzar figured case closed; end of story. Certainly, there was no way for them to survive, and live to (testify) about it. But the unfathomable is fathomable with the LORD our God. Nebuchadnezzar exclaimed, "Didn't we cast three bound men into the fire? Now, I see four ('unbound' men) walking around in the flames, and the fourth looks like a son of God." (Daniel 3: 92)

As would later be the case with the prophet Daniel when he was thrown into a den of lions, the God of Heaven has a way of intervening man's affairs, in such a way, that people are left awestruck. Scripture says, "The fire had no power over them (the three captives); not a hair on their head was singed." (Daniel 3: 95)

But what about those individuals who find themselves the butt of demeaning comments, derogatory epithets, racial slurs, and harassing taunts, daily? What about them? I wish I could offer a better answer than the one presented in Scripture; but I can't. The Judean captives told the king; "Even if our God does not save us from the blazing furnace, and from your (wicked) hand, know for sure, your Majesty, that we will never bow down to your gods, nor worship the statue (the Colossus) that you've set up." (Daniel 3: 17)

King Nebuchadnezzar represents a type of antagonist, and the prophet Daniel is a type of Christ-figure. In calling attention to the sacred vessels stolen from the Holy Temple, Daniel was echoing the God of Heaven's resolve to retrieve and restore, you and I, "vessels", that the Adversary had attempted to separate from God, the Master Potter.

If the chasm between belief and doubt could be illustrated by way of allegory, let's use the differing explanations for how and why Daniel escaped the perils of the lion's den.

As Daniel was being lifted out, a spectator remarked, "Daniel wasn't eaten (did not die) because the lions must not have been hungry."

People of faith perceive (discern) things differently.

Referring to his rescue (deliverance) by the God of Heaven, Daniel aptly stated;

> *"My God sent an angel to shut the mouths of the lions; I have found innocence in His sight."*
> *(Daniel 6: 21-22)*

Praise God!

After-all, it was Daniel's interaction with the angel Gabriel (sealed-up in a book-scroll until the end-time) that provides a prophetic-glimpse of the biblical-timeline.

"The one who appeared like a man, told me, "At that time Michael (Guardian of Israel) will stand up for the descendants of your people. And it will be a time of sever trouble and duress, unlike anything nations had ever known, previously. Everyone written in the Book, will be rescued. Many who are asleep in the ground will wake up; some to life eternal, (but) others shall wake to lasting shame and disgrace. Those who are wise (having divine-understanding) will shine like the brightness on

the horizon; those who lead people to righteousness will shine like stars forever." (Daniel 12: 1-3)

Seeds of Expectation

We do our utmost to remain "in Christ" (the Word). For, not unlike the time of Nehemiah, people are wanting (hoping for) something more.

In the parable of the Prodigal Son, the father told his eldest son to embrace his younger brother's return; for it equated to a huge gain for all concerned, not a loss.

"Son, you are always with me; everything I have is yours'. But this brother of yours, who was dead, has come back to life—he was lost, but now he is found." (Luke 15: 32)

About the impetuous carnal-driven son, who'd demanded (and received) his share of the inheritance, and squandered it living the fast life, Scripture says, "He finally came to his senses, and realized how good he had it at home, under his father's roof.

Thus, he went about rehearsing what he would say should he decide to return home.

> *"I'll go at once to my father, and I'll say to him,*
> *'Father, I have sinned against heaven and you.*
> *I don't deserve to be called your son anymore.'"*
> *(Luke 15: 18-19)*

Scripture describes the scene of reconciliation;

"While he (the son) was still at a distance, his father saw him, and felt compassion for him. He ran to his son, and put his arms around him, and kissed him." (Luke 15: 20-23)

The father was just happy to have his son back.

Foundation of Spirit

Bravery is often associated with acts of heroism during some sort of combat-situation. But we recognize another form of heroism and courage that "flies under the radar", despite the daily salvos of accusation and condemnation.

To read a broadcasting company's "disclaimer" preceding or following Christian programming is dare I say, irritating; For it usually, states something like the "views expressed by the following program do not reflect the views of "this or that media company", nor its' employees." Isn't that presumptuous on the media company's part? Frankly, it's a demonstration of what people of faith are up against, daily, weekly, yearly. Despite all the corporate $$$ spent on bandwidth, the LORD still owns the airwaves!

Of course, people are concerned with putting bread on the table. But why not supplement that with what is priceless, that money can't buy?

"Listen! Whoever is thirsty, come to the water! Whoever has no money can come and eat! You do not have to pay; it's free. Why do you spend

money on that which cannot nourish (you spiritually); why spend your wages on what cannot satisfy you? spend money on bread that doesn't satisfy." (Isaiah 55: 1-2)

The LORD uses a person's willingness to believe as if it (faith) were soil being prepared for planting.

> *"I send out My Word ("Jesus") like rain and snow coming down from the heavens to water the earth. I send it (My Word) out, and it always produces fruit." (Isaiah 55: 10-11)*

As much as we'd prefer doing things the "old fashioned way" (by earning it), we are urged to avail ourselves to something new; possibly, unprecedented.

The LORD says;

> *"See! I am doing something new! It (a great marvel that eclipses what came before) springs forth; do you not perceive it?" (Isaiah 43: 19)*

As declared through the LORD's mouthpiece (the prophet Isaiah);

> *"He (God) has sent me to bring good news to the afflicted, to bind up (comfort) the brokenhearted, and proclaim liberty to captives, and freedom to prisoners." (Isaiah 61: 1)*

As delivered by Jesus, the Messiah;

"I have told you all this while I am with you. The Advocate, the Holy Spirit, that the Father will send (advocating on behalf of Christ's purpose), will remind you of everything I have told you. My peace (the fullness of the Messianic blessing) I give you; not as the world gives do I give to you. Do not let your hearts be troubled." (John 14: 25-27)

The Discovery

As an archaeologist seeks to discover evidence of an ancient temple's existence, the Body of Christ continues to be "unearthed" as proof to those who believe.

The Holy One of Israel, God, the Creator of Heaven and earth, "reversed the curse", which He, Himself, had leveled at the ground ("adamah") all those generations ago.

Jesus absorbed the divine-penalty (under the Law) so that we, the descendants of Adam, might be restored to "right-relationship" (reconciled) with God our Maker.

In keeping with the already established principle for atonement, God provided.

> *"The life of any creature is in its blood. (So), I have given this blood to you so you can make peace with Me (be right with God) on the altar; (sacrificial) blood is required for the forgiveness of sins." (Leviticus 17: 11)*

As the anointed David (the name David in Hebrew, means "beloved") aptly noted;

> "Blessed is the man (person) who's disobedience is forgiven; whose sin is pardoned." (Psalms 32: 1)

The life, death, resurrection, and ascension of Jesus ("Son of David") serve as "ladder-like steps" in God's salvation plan.

> "At the moment Jesus yielded up his spirit (breathed his last breath), "the curtain in the Temple tore in two, from top to bottom. And there was an earthquake causing rocks to split apart and graves to open. Many, who'd been dead and buried, were raised to life." (Matthew 27: 51-52)

The "anomaly with anointing" embodied the elements of water (purification), oil (sanctification), bread from heaven (provision), and blood (atonement).

The Crimson Thread

The biblical tapestry is woven through unlikely figures and events. Who but God could position Pharaoh to produce an exodus, and open a "gateway" through a dead end?

The link between Moses, "one drawn from water", and Jesus, "one sanctified in blood", is like an "intersection of bridges";

the horizontal passage to the Promised Land, fused with the vertical ascent to the Kingdom of Heaven.

The God of the Old Testament, and God of the New Testament are one and the same; full of loving-kindness, compassion, and mercy (grace).

> "Praise the LORD, my soul; never forget all the good He has done. He is the One who forgives your sins, the One who heals all your diseases, the One who rescues your life from the pit, the One crowning you with mercy and compassion, the One who fills your life with blessings so that you become young again like an eagle." (Psalms 103: 2-5)

> "The LORD is compassionate, merciful, and patient; He always ready to forgive." (Ps. 103: 8) He has not treated us as we deserve; nor has He paid us back for our wrong-doing." (Psalms 103: 9-10)

> "As a father has compassion for his children, so the LORD has compassion for those who fear Him. He knows what we are made of; we are (merely) dust." (Psalms 103: 13-14)

The LORD uses a person's willingness to believe as if it (faith) were soil being prepared for planting.

> "I send out My Word ("Jesus") like rain and snow coming down from the heavens to water

the earth. I send it (My Word) out, and it always produces fruit." (Isaiah 55: 10-11)

To give you an idea of how stereotypes and preconceptions can unjustly cloud a person's receptivity to all that God has in store, I avoided reading anything written in the Book of Tobit (which follows the Book of Nehemiah in the Apocrypha) because, frankly, the name "Tobit" wasn't Jewish enough for my "Jewish sensibilities." But, guess what? Tobit was a devout Jew from the upper Galilee region of Israel, who happened to have the misfortune of being among the Jewish exiles deported to Nineveh.

> *"I, Tobit, have walked all the days of my life on paths of fidelity and righteousness. I performed charitable deeds for my kindred, and my people who, like myself, have been taken captive to Nineveh by the Assyrians." (Tobit 1: 3)*
>
> *"I, alone, from the house of Naphtali, refrained from offering sacrifices on the hilltops to the (idolatrous) calf which king Jeroboam had set up in the city of Dan." (Tobit 1: 5)*
>
> *"I, alone, went to Jerusalem, as prescribed by Law, bringing with me first-fruits of my crops, and the firstlings of my flock, and presented them to the priests, Aaron's sons, at the site of the holy altar." (Tobit 1: 6-7)*

Tobit's account is particularly inspiring. For as recorded in writings included in the Hebrew canonical books, and not,

God, the Holy One of Israel, hears (inhabits) the prayers of His people. The angel Raphael explains (to Tobit) the purpose of his visit.

> *"I was sent to put you to the test; but, at the same time, God sent me to heal you (Tobit) and your daughter-in-law, Sarah. When you prayed, it was I who presented the record of your prayer before the Glory of the Lord." (Tobit 12: 12)*

> *"Do not fear. Peace be with you! Bless God Most High, now and forever. As for me, when I was with you, I was doing God's will. Bless the LORD every day in praise and song." (Tobit 12: 17-18)*

> *"Look, now I am ascending to the One who sent me. Write down all that has happened to you." (Tobit 12: 20)*

The Son, the Father of the Man

For all the "closed doors" at ground level, the Good News garnered applause and celebration in the heavens above.

> *"On the eve of Jesus' birth, an angel of the Lord appeared among some shepherds outside the village (of Bethlehem), and the radiance of the Lord's glory surrounded them. The angel said, 'Do not be afraid; for behold I proclaim*

to you good news that will bring great joy to all people! Today, in the City of David, a savior has been born for you, who is the Messiah, and Lord.' Suddenly, the angel was joined by a multitude of heavenly hosts; praising God, and saying, 'Glory to God in the highest, and peace (on earth) to those on whom His favor rests."
(Luke 2: 10-14)

The followers of Jesus believed He was the Messiah; the anointed One sent by God to redeem the Children of Israel.

As an example of the power of the Word of God, let's revisit the significance of Jesus' immersion (baptism by John) into the waters of the River Jordan.

"When Jesus came up out of the water, the heavens opened to Him. He saw the Spirit of God descending like a dove upon Him. Suddenly a voice came from Heaven, announcing, 'This is My beloved Son in whom I AM well pleased." (Matthew 3: 16)

Upon securing the "identifying-signature" as the beloved Son of God Most High, Jesus was prepared to confront the adversary pf the seed of Abraham.

> *"He (Jesus) fasted forty days and forty nights; and afterwards, he was hungry. The Tempter approached Jesus, and provocatively premised the attack with the phrase, "If you are the Son of God", then command these stones to become bread." (Matthew 4: 3)*

Jesus was unfazed. He thwarted the attack by citing the Word of God (specifically, Scripture verses from the Book of Deuteronomy).

> *"The Tanakh says (It is written), 'Man shall not live by bread alone; but by every word that comes from the mouth of God'." (Matthew 4: 3-4)*

After three failed attempts to draw (lure) Jesus the "beloved" Son away from his position of "covenantal one-ness" with the Father, the Accuser disappeared from the scene.

Scripture notes, "And then ministering angels came, and took care of him (Yeshua)." (Matthew 4: 11)

Could it be any clearer? The Word of God is purposed as a sword and a shield.

> *"Put on the Lord's righteousness as a breastplate. And on your feet wear the readiness that comes with the Good News." (Ephesians 6: 14-15)*

It's fair to say that believers learn to "wage peace."

> *"No one who is engaged in warfare, gets overly entangled (bogged down) with the affairs of the world." (2 Timothy 2: 4)*

The System

The sacrificial-system had its' share of limitations, given human nature combined with the limited number of unblemished bulls, he-goats, and lambs to go around.

Thankfully, God provided Himself "an offering", which in effect, canceled (or revised) the old way of doing things.

The parallels between Abraham, "the father of nations" placing his son, Isaac (his "only" son) on the altar, and God the Father orchestrating a virtual replay of the "binding of Isaac" at the very same location (on Mount Moriah) is not something we can shrug off as happenstance. I don't speak Hebrew, but I've heard it said that Abraham's reply to Isaac's question, "Father! Here's the fire and the wood for the burnt offering, but where is the sheep", in the original Hebrew, can be understood as Abraham telling Isaac, "God will provide Himself, the sheep (or lamb) for the burnt offering." In other words, the "binding of Isaac" (on the altar), and the fastening of Jesus on the wooden cross, are totally related events. What's more, Abraham had named the place, "Yahweh-yireh", meaning, "the LORD will provide". Are believers supposed to pretend not to discern the obvious? The LORD our God absolutely provided! And the "divine-exchange" took the human element out of the equation.

In Old Testament times, blessings were dispensed, or withheld, according to the high priest's "standing with God." In other words, if the sitting high priest had done wrong in God's sight, the entire community suffered. Fortunately, with Jesus as the High Priest, "eternally-extraordinaire", people of faith have the blessed assurance that no regime change, not alteration in political-leadership, nor the whims and fickleness of human nation, negates their standing with God. For God views you through the rose-colored blood-stained lens of Yeshua's righteousness (finished work on the Cross of Calvary).

Given that we are spoken for by God, you may at times feel like you're swimming upstream, instead of "going with the flow" of public opinion. I mean the "powers-that-be" seem bent on reducing people to a formulaic-equation, and/or a ratio (algorithm) of chance and probability. Be not obliged to sink to the lowest common denominator, "because everyone else is doing it."

The slogans, and promotional campaigns of the world beckon you and I to "live everyday as if it's your last", or, why not "throw caution to the wind", "you only live once."

And yet we are advised by God;

> *"Since he clings to Me, I will rescue him. I will raise him high because he has acknowledged My Name." (Psalms 91: 14)*

Whistle-blower or Trumpeter

There was the prophet Jeremiah, smack-dab in the middle of Jerusalem, with a self-fashioned wooden yoke worn around his neck (to symbolize the prospects of captivity in Babylon), questioning the "leadership" of the religious elite.

"Let not a wise man gloat (or glory) in his wisdom. Let not the mighty man glory in his might. Let not the rich man tout (glory) in his riches; (instead) let him (or her) boast in this alone; that he (or she) truly knows Me. I AM the LORD of justice, of righteousness, and of unfailing loving-kindness." (Jeremiah 9: 23-24)

"Those who forsake You will be put to shame; (for) they've forsaken the LORD, the source of living waters." (Jeremiah 17: 13)

"My people have done two things wrong; they have abandoned Me, the fountain of life-giving water, and they've dug their own wells, (cracked cisterns) that cannot hold water." (Jeremiah 2: 13)

"When you look for Me, I (the LORD) will let you find Me. When you seek Me with all your heart, I (the LORD) will let you find Me; and I will change your lot in life—gathering you up from all the places (nations) to which I had banished (dispersed) you. I will bring you back to the place from which I had sent you into exile." (Jeremiah 29: 13-14)

You could say that God, Creator of all there is, and ever-will-be, utilizes "Jacob's (Israel's) journey, and the dispersal of Judeans from the land of Israel (Diaspora), as a type of foreshadowing of the Creator's overall restoration plan. For just as the people of Israel (along with the so-called, "lost tribes of Israel) have been brought back to the land of their forefathers, so shall God Most High, maker of Heaven and earth, draw (reconcile) people and nations to Himself.

> *"I (the LORD) will gather you from all the nations and places where I scattered (dispersed. or banished) you. And I will bring you back to the place from I sent you into exile." (Jeremiah 29: 14)*

> *"I will bring them back from the distant corners of the earth. Tears of joy will stream down their faces, and I, the Lord, will lead them home with great care. I am Israel's father, and Ephraim is my oldest child." (Jeremiah 31: 9)*

Joseph's son Ephraim was not the elder son; so, for Jeremiah to refer to him as "Israel's (Jacob's) oldest child", beckons us to think "outside-the-box." Recall, when Joseph positioned his son Manasseh in such a way that Jacob's hand would hover over the firstborn son (Manasseh) bestowing the anticipated blessing. But Jacob crossed his hands, which, in effect, gave the coveted blessing of the firstborn to Ephraim (not Manasseh). Joseph was taken back by what seemed to him, as a mistake, on his father's part. "Father, this is not right; the other one (Manasseh) is the firstborn. Lay your right hand on his head!" (Genesis 48: 18)

But Jacob refused to make the requested change; telling his son Joseph, "I know what I am doing, my son. That one (Manasseh) too shall become a people; but his younger brother

Ephraim representing Israel) will surpass him." (Genesis 48: 18-19)

> *"The days are coming', says Adonai (the LORD), "when I will establish over the House of Israel and the House of Judah, a new covenant. It will not be like the covenant I made with their ancestors, because they, for their part, did not remain faithful to the agreement. Hence, this is the new covenant I will make with the House of Israel: 'I will place My Law within them, writing it upon their hearts." (Jeremiah 31: 31-33)*

The Holy One of Israel had told Jeremiah;

> *"If you speak words that are worthy, you will be my spokesman. You are to influence them, but do not let them influence you!" (Jeremiah 15: 1)*

> *"Write, for yourself, in a book, all the words I have spoken to you. The days are coming when I shall bring back the captives of my people." (Jeremiah 30: 1-4)*

The LORD asked me;

> *"What do you see, Jeremiah? I answered, 'I see a branch of the almond tree.' The LORD responded, 'You have seen well; for I AM watching over My Word to carry it out." (Jeremiah 1: 11-11-12)*

The almond tree begins blooms in late winter. The almond tree symbolizes a blooming and flourishes even in the "dead of winter"; a symbol of resurrection.

> *"Blessed is the man who trusts in the LORD, whose hope is in the LORD God. He shall be like a tree that's planted by the waters, having roots that spread out by the river. It's (his) leaves will be green, and it (he) won't stop yielding fruit." (Jeremiah 17: 7-8)*

The Sighted Blind Man

In the ancient world, people were under the impression that physical-malady and defect were due to some sort of wrong-doing (sin) committed by the affected person; or a product of a generational-curse.

All (of us) have sinned; and all of us fall short of the glory of God.

The disciples questioned Jesus about the causal-factors for "congenital-blindness"; asking, "Why was this man born blind (they assumed the condition was due to sin)?"

Jesus set them straight on the matter; "Neither he, nor his parents, sinned. He (the man) was born blind, so the power of God could be seen in him." (John 9: 2-3)

The prescription-pad issued by the Great Physician (God... Eternal) serves as the healing-salve for the affliction of man's soul (and the remedy for a case of spiritual-deadness).

> *"I (the LORD) will set the captives free (from the waterless pit), because of the blood that sealed My promise. So, return to your fortress, you, prisoners of hope. Today, I (the LORD) will return (compensate) you double (the blessings)." (Zechariah 9: 11-12)*

> *"Many people and nations will come to seek the LORD in Jerusalem; and there they'll ask the LORD for a blessing. The LORD of Armies says: 'Ten people from every language among the nations will take hold of the garment of a Jew; saying, 'Let us go with you (to Jerusalem), because we have heard God is with you (God-with-you, Emmanuel)." (Zechariah 8: 22-23)*

The blood of the Paschal Lamb gave God "legal-cause" to stamp the sin-debt incurred through Adam and Eve, "paid in full."

> *"I (the LORD) have given you the blood to make atonement for yourselves on the altar. (For), it's the blood, as life, that makes (obtains) atonement." (Leviticus 17: 11)*

Rejoice! For the generational curse which had spiraled down the Family Tree of Man (since the debacle in Eden) ran into the Last, and the First, domino standing.

Jesus, as "the Way, the Truth, and the Life" is the God-prescribed anecdote for snake (serpent) bite; the curative remedy for the malady of spiritual-blindness (deadness).

> *"For God so loved the world that He gave His only Son, that whoever believes in Him will not perish, but have eternal live." (John 3: 16)*

Generally, human nature likes being the one who lights up a room, the one who hits a walk-off home run at the end of a game, the one who throws a last second touchdown pass with time ticking down; but when it comes to the ways of God, be prepared to take a back seat. For the Kingdom of God operates on an entirely different reward system.

And for all the "closed doors" at ground level, the Good News garnered applause and celebration in the heavens above.

> *"On the eve of Jesus' birth, an angel of the Lord appeared among some shepherds outside the village (of Bethlehem), and the radiance of the Lord's glory surrounded them. The angel said, 'Do not be afraid; for behold I proclaim to you good news that will bring great joy to all people! Today, in the City of David, a savior has been born for you, who is the Messiah, and Lord.' Suddenly, the angel was joined by a multitude of heavenly hosts; praising God, and saying, 'Glory to God in the highest, and peace (on earth) to those on whom His favor rests." (Luke 2: 10-14)*

In Christ, there's "amplification" of the true yearnings of our soul. Thus, we are empowered to rearrange our priorities.

No longer are we bound by carnal-pursuits geared for leaving a "carbon-footprint."

Manna para El Alma

The Word of God may not directly put "bread on the table", but it does amount to "credit in Heaven", and rewards yet to come.

> *"The Son of Man has come to save that which was lost. "If a man (shepherd, or shepherdess) has a 100 sheep, does he not leave the 99 to seek the one that went astray? Similarly, I guarantee you; when he finds the one sheep that was lost, he's happier about it, than the 99 sheep that hadn't strayed. In the same way, the Son of Man, came to save (restore) that which was lost." (Matthew 18: 12-14)*

> *"I (the LORD), will search for, and find My sheep; and like a shepherd looking for his scattered flock, I (the LORD) will bring them back home." (Ezekiel 34: 11-13)*

The link between Moses, "one drawn from water", and Jesus, "one sanctified in blood", is like an "intersection of bridges"; the horizontal passage to the Promised Land, fused with the vertical ascent to the Kingdom of Heaven.

Passing the Torch

It was at the river's edge (along the banks of the Jordan) that the mantel or torch was passed.

> *"He (Jesus) must become greater, and I (John) must become less. He who comes from above is above all. Whereas, he who is of earth-dust ('adamah') speaks only from an earthly perspective (with limited understanding)."*
> *(John 3: 30-31)*

Generally, human nature likes being the one who lights up a room, the one who hits a walk-off home run at the end of a game, the one who throws a last second touchdown pass with time ticking down; but when it comes to the ways of God, be prepared to take a back seat. For the Kingdom of God operates on an entirely different reward system.

Confidence derives from the Word.

> *"You didn't choose me, I chose you; commissioning you to go and bear fruit." (John 15: 16)*

The Messenger

The arch-angel Gabriel (whose name in Hebrew translates, "strong man (of God)", or "God is My strength" came to the Zechariah, while he was dutifully serving in the Temple.

It is noted that both Zechariah and his wife Elisheva (Elizabeth) were descendants of the priestly line of Aaron; and that they zealously observed the commandments of God." (Luke 1: 5-6)

As careful as they were in adhering the Mosaic Law, a moment of doubt carried repercussions

Note; Gabriel had last appeared (to Daniel in Babylon) announcing, "70 weeks of years" (490 years) would remain after the Babylonian exile, until the coming of the Messiah."

The angel of the LORD got Zechariah's full attention, informing him; "I am Gabriel, who stands before God. I was sent to you, and to announce good news. Yet, you questioned if what I have told you was possible. Now (on account of doubt) you'll be rendered speechless, unable to talk, until these things come to pass (take place)." (Luke 1: 19)

For a priest "without a voice" would be something like a king without a throne, a Levite without the Tabernacle to maintain, and a prophet with a message to deliver.

Harkening to the "voice of the angel" was central to the fate (or destiny) of many in the land of Israel.

> *"The neighbors of Zechariah were aware of the mercy that God had shown Elisheva (Elizabeth), for she'd long been barren, but at last, she conceived a child, and had given birth. So when guests gathered (on the eighth day following the boy's birth), to share in the celebratory joy of the day of circumcision,*

> attendees discussed "the naming" of the child. boy. Some favored the name 'Zechariah' (obviously, after his father), but Elizabeth, remembering the words of the angel Gabriel, spoke up; 'No! He will be called 'John.' The assembled guests were perplexed, saying, 'But no one among your relatives has that name.' They all looked to Zechariah to settle the issue. And that he did! The "priest without a voice" motioned for a writing tablet; and on it, he wrote, 'John is his name.' (Luke 1: 57-63)

Scripture states;

> "Immediately his mouth was opened; his tongue freed (Zechariah was no longer tongue-tied)." (Luke 1: 64-65)

Presently, we, the people, we, the nation, need someone who's called in the spirit of Elijah; with the God-inspired vibrancy to move the hearts of fathers to their children. He will change the hearts of disobedient people, so they'll be receptive to godly wisdom. And in this way, he shall prepare the way for the coming of the LORD." (Luke 1: 17)

> "There was a man in Jerusalem whose name was Simon (Shimon). He was a righteous man who eagerly awaited the Consolation of Israel (meaning, the comforting of Israel by the LORD). The Holy Spirit was upon Shimon, and He (the Spirit) revealed to Shimon that he wouldn't die before seeing the Messiah. One day, prompted

by the Holy Spirit, Shimon went to the Holy Temple, where the parents of the 'Savior-to-be' just so happened to be preparing their son to be ceremonially consecrated to the LORD. And when Shimon saw the child, he took him his arms, and pronounced a blessing; saying, 'Adonai (God), according to your word, your servant is now at peace. I have seen your Yeshu'ah (salvation); a light that will bring revelation to Gentiles (non-Jews), and glory for your people Israel." (Luke 2: 27-32)

Shimon pronounced a blessing on Mary and Joseph; and prophetically added,

> "Behold this child, who will cause many in Israel to fall and to rise. He will become a sign whom people will speak against; and moreover, a sword will pierce your heart, also. All this will happen in order to reveal the innermost thoughts of many people." (Luke 2: 34-35)

Scripture records;

> "Eight days after his birth, the child was christened with the name that the angel of the LORD (Gabriel) had revealed to Joseph (Yosef) and Mary (Miryam). At the proper time according to Jewish Law, Mary and Joseph brought their infant son to the Temple to be presented to the LORD. It was there that Simeon had the prayer of his lifetime, answered. And, it was there that Anna, an

elderly prophetess, a descendant of Phanuel, who Scripture describes as pious to the point, that she never left the Temple courtyards, worshiping day and night, praying and fasting." (A widow for 84 years). Upon seeing Mary and Joseph, Anna approached them, and she spontaneously began thanking God." (Luke 2: 36-38)

Anna proceeded to tell others (who'd been anxiously waiting to be set free) about Yeshua." (Luke 2: 36-38)

In Christ, we seek the things above.

"As He is ('beloved') so too are we, in this world." (1 John 4: 17)

In these days when vitriolic-rhetoric and derogatory-language seems to be ratcheting up into some sort of crescendo, we refuse to sing-along to that discordant bombast.

In solidarity; "Todos somos Ana."

Detour to Destiny

I have heard it said that "there are two kinds of people in the world", those who like Neil Diamond (the music of Neil Diamond), and those who do not." For me, a recent trip to Israel, rendered differences in musical tastes a mute-point. After-all, the Great Composer's grand orchestration culminated there, on Redemption's Hill, at the foot of the Cross.

Slightly confused, Daniel stared intently at the ATM machine's screen, which was full of Hebrew letters. He figured there must be an "English-language" button somewhere, among the swaying, seemingly pictographic-characters of the Hebrew language. The tour guide must have interpreted the blank perplexed look on Daniel' face as an "invitation"; for before Daniel could even ask for assistance, Mr. Levy (the tour guide) offered to help.

Daniel, being out of his element, like "a fish out of water", uncomfortably deferred to Mr. Levy's all-too-helpful expertise in navigating the screen of the ATM machine on Nablus Street. Before Daniel could even contemplate the ramifications, or mindfully weigh the amount to pay for services rendered, the tour guide's hand swooped, and struck the 600 shekel-button on the ATM machine. Daniel was reduced to a helpless spectator as the ATM machine spit out one, two, three, five, a total of six, hundred-shekel notes.

The so-called "natural order of things", etiquette had been cast aside.

(Earlier that same day...)

Daniel and Jerome walked toward the Jaffa Gate on the northwest corner of Jerusalem's Old City, intending only to get acquainted with the usual walking route to the Temple Mount. However, our informal "meet and greet" the Old City, suddenly became a dilemma of what seemed "biblical-proportion." Out of nowhere, a man wearing a baseball hat, was in front of us, presenting himself as an indispensable guide of the Old City. Characterizing, Mr. Levy (that was not his real name) as a great salesman would be a gross understatement. Positioning himself in front of us, so we could not proceed further, he confidently inquired, "Where are you going? It's Shabbat, nothing will be open. Besides, it is better to enter by going down the road; and take a back door into the city." He grinned, and added, "And besides, you don't want to go by yourself. You will get lost. I'm a very good tour guide. In fact, I once showed Neil Diamond around, when he was here on a concert tour." He pulled out his wallet, and sure enough, there was a photo of Mr. Levy with Neil Diamond.

Jerome, looking upwards, pondered within himself, had we not come to Israel, Jerusalem, specifically, seeking, praying, hoping for "a conformational-sign?" It was clear as God asking Abraham to envision his descendants as being as numerous as the stars in the sky; the only thing now standing in our way was a daytime sky which concealed their existence. With that in mind, I, we, said "Yes!"

Mr. Levy led us through the narrow streets with the precision of a fighter pilot. He matter-of-factly, guided us to the relevant sites in the Old City; at times entering us through exits, by-passing lines of tourists.

It was almost like we were walking on air, humming along to Mr. Levy's rendition of "Crackling Rosie" (from the Neil Diamond catalogue of music). We'd navigated the narrow passageways, bobbing and weaving through the various sectors of the Old City.

(Present time…)

Mr. Levy had repeatedly reminded us, "Money comes and goes; it is not important. Family, friends and the relationships we forge in life is what matters." Now, the whirlwind tour had reached its' inevitable conclusion. All that remained was the issue of payment. As it turned out, an ATM machine on Nablus Street, positioned a few hundred yards from the site popularly known as the Garden Tomb, played a role in framing the all the all too real dual vying for supremacy in the minds of men. In a world beholden to numbers ($$$), we're challenge not to let monetary-issues put a damper on spiritual-truths. Thankfully, the "currency of redemption", namely, the blood of Christ, amounts to "credits in Heaven."

Rolling Away the Stone

The precise location of the burial-tomb in which Joseph of Arimathea, a member of the Jewish High Council, placed the linen-wrapped body of Jesus, is not entirely clear. There are two competing narratives, one more favorable to the Church of the Holy Sepulcher, and the other, the Garden Tomb, as being the escarpment called the "Place of the Skull" (Golgotha), the place where Jesus was crucified, and subsequently placed in a burial cave.

Thankfully, the Good News surpasses any denominational differences; (for) "He is Risen!"

> *"Early on the first day of the week (Sunday), Mary of Magdala went to the tomb, where the stone, which had covered the tomb's entrance, no longer in place. Alarmed, she ran back to*

Simon Peter, telling him and the others, 'They've taken the Lord out of the tomb'." (John 20: 1-2)

"The disciples came to see whether Mary's report was accurate. Peter and the other disciple went to the site of the burial-cave. Scripture says, "The other disciple ran faster than Peter, and arrived at the tomb, first. He bent down and saw the burial cloths there. But he did not go inside. Soon Peter arrived, and he proceeded into the tomb. Once inside, Peter saw the burial-linens, and he also saw the cloth which had covered Jesus' head; now, it was rolled up, and in a separate place." (John 20: 3-7)

In Luke's account of the same scene, we read; "The women ((Mary Magdalene, Joanna, and Mary, the mother of James) were puzzling over the fact the stone was no longer covering the tomb's entrance, when two men (angelic-figures) in clothes that were as bright as lightening suddenly were standing there with them. The scene terrified the women, and they fell (prostrate) to the ground." What the angel said next highlights man's propensity to get so bogged down "in the details" that we're apt we lose sight of the big picture; unable to see "the forest through the trees."

"Why do you seek the living among the dead?' (Luke 24: 4-6)

Speak Life!

My father had a non-speaking role in a 1930's James Cagney movie titled Angels with Dirty Faces. I remember that in a riveting scene near the end of the film, the parish priest visits the character played by James Cagney, who's in prison, on death row. The priest makes an impassioned plea to the condemned man (Cagney) to do something that's totally contrary to his public persona; to act cowardly when walking to the electric chair. The priest makes the request, so that the next day news won't be reporting how won't be reporting that the criminal had remained brazenly defiant to the very end. The parish priest was concerned about the impressionable minds of a group of neighborhood youths ("the Dead-End Kids"), who already viewed the larger-than-life thug-persona as something to emulate; the father of the Church didn't want the next day news about the execution to add fodder that might glamourize a life of crime. Cagney's character faced an agonizing decision. Would he choose to swallow his pride for the sake of the kids (the greater good), or would he choose to maintain the "tough guy" to the end?

I know it was only a movie, but the ending in which Cagney, I mean, Cagney's character, broke down and cried like a baby on his walk to the death chamber, left me wanting something more. What if the Screenwriter Most High, the Author of Life, wrote "death's obituary"; and the ending was only the beginning?

> *"The LORD, God Almighty, has put every enemy under foot; the last enemy to be neutralized is death." (1 Corinthians 15: 25-26)*

Faith and Football

One hesitates to rehash "old news", but for those who remember, the phenomenon known as "Tebow-mania", was something to behold. Sport pundits and commentators had a field day criticizing Tim Tebow's "flawed delivery" (of a football). In a world that puts a premium on numbers, it's refreshing to witness events which are "off the charts" of the statisticians.

In the 2012 NFL Wild Card playoff game between the Denver Broncos and Pittsburg Steelers (won by the Broncos, 29-23, in overtime), faith and football converged into a glorious moment in time. Tebow first pass in overtime was caught by a receiver, who then sprinted into the end zone for a touchdown.

Who can argue with divine synchronicity? Two years previous, on draft day 2010, the Denver Broncos positioned themselves to select both players, Demaryius Thomas with the 22nd pick, and Tebow, three spots later, at # 25.

Tebow has been criticized for "wearing his faith on his sleeve" (in his eye-black). Why? Faith is like storehouse of credits in Heaven.

> *"God so loved the world that He gave His only begotten Son; so whoever believes in him will have life, everlasting." (John 3: 16)*

Tim's pass in overtime came to rest in the hands of a receiver who just so happens to share a birthday with the One known as the "finisher of our faith."

His game day stat-line confounded the most ardent of statisticians. Firstly, the game itself, was being played three years from the day Tim Tebow, quarterback of the Florida Gators, chose to scribe "3: 16" in his eye-black, for the collegiate National Championship Game.

Stat-line for the game:
His passing yards totaled 316
He averaged 3.16 rushing yards
He averaged 31.6 yards per completion.
And Denver's time of possession that day totaled 31: 06 minutes.

> *Timothy R. Tebow — Born 8/14/1987,*
> *Makati City, Philippines*

Be encouraged to pray for all people.

> *"I urge you to pray for all people; and in presenting your petitions, plead the LORD's mercy be upon them; and give thanks." (1 Timothy 2: 1)*

Of the tragic ironies occurring in the lead up to the Holocaust was that Hitler's obsession with the notion of a so-called, "master-race" (Aryan or "white supremacy"), resulted in an array of dictatorial mandates in the period leading up to the Holocaust. Included on the list of prohibitions was a ban on Jews donating blood. You would have thought someone would have sat him down, and forcefully pointed out that a Jew, a descendant of the savior-figure Noah, had donated the requisite God-approved blood type, having the power to save humanity from itself (devices of its own making).

The Good News is bad news for the adversary.

In reading excerpts from the Book of Enoch, you come away with an understanding that a crime was perpetrated against God's creation. From that perspective, the Bible is a guiding-light (a Jeremiah type "sign-post") directing you and I home. And just as Daniel called attention to the sacred-vessels stolen (by the forces of the king of Babylon), the Holy Spirit is constantly at work, "calling us out" from under the pharaoh-like "ruler of the world", while simultaneously, lighting the "narrow-gate" pathway home.

> *"Now, you are no longer strangers (resident-aliens); instead you are fellow-citizens of the holy ones, members of the household of God."*
> *(Ephesians 2: 19)*

When you dig into the subject (which invariably means familiarizing yourself with the Word), truth emerges. As Jesus explained to the Samaritan woman at "Jacob's well"; "We (Jews) worship what we know, because salvation is from the Jews." Yeshua's statement was not so much a statement about ethnicity, tribal-affiliation, or "chosen-status", as it was a shout-out to the "closeness" that Hebrew-speaking people have with the will of God. In fact, instance, all the biblical-names (Adam to Noah's son Methuselah) preceding the incident at the Tower of Babel convey meaning in the Semitic-tongue of Hebrew (example: "Lamech named his son Noah, saying, 'this one will bring us relief from the toil of our hands, in the very ground the LORD has cursed." (Genesis 5: 29)

You could say, by name alone, Noah, was called to be a curse-breaking "vessel of God." Similarly, people of faith have a spirit-powered ark-like vessel with upward-mobility.

The New Song

To wait on the LORD is not easy, especially in a dog-eat-dog world. It's all too easy to, inadvertently, "get out in front" of God's timing.

Metaphorically-speaking, we are all in that same boat, but with one caveat. To be "in Christ" is to have embarked on a voyage that promises to take you to the next level.

Upon reading how the biblical-storyline ends, does it really matter whether you call it the First Coming, or the Second?

The wait is well worth it.

> "No longer will nations take up the sword against one another; no longer will they train for war. So, House of Jacob, and all peoples and nations, let us walk in the light of the LORD." (Isaiah 2: 4-5)

In the Book of Revelation, we read:

> "The four living creatures and the 24 elders bowed before Him. They sang a new song

having these words: 'You (the Lamb) are worthy to take the scroll, break its seals, and open it. For you were slaughtered, and your blood purchased (redeemed) many, from every tribe, language, people (ethnicity), and nation." (Revelation 5: 8-9)

The "New Song" sung in the heavens above drowns out the "same old un-inspired tune." Whatever discordant notes were struck in the past, now harmonize in the Great Composer's grand symphony.

"The Creator of Heaven and earth, through the body of Christ, demonstrated His Infinite (multi-faceted) wisdom and authority to the rulers and principalities in the realms above." (Ephesians 3: 10)

"And a loud vice from the throne said: "See! The glorious presence of God is with mankind. He will dwell with mankind; they shall be His people, and He, Himself ('God-with-them') will be their God. And He will wipe away every tear from their eyes." (Revelation 21: 3-4)

"Then the angel showed me the river of the water of life, flowing from the throne of God, and the Lamb. And between the main avenue and the river, was the Tree of Life, the leaves of which were for healing the nations—no longer will there be any curses." (Revelation 22: 1-3)

"As God's partners, we beg you not to reject this message of God's mercy (kindness and compassion). The LORD says, 'I heard you, and on the day of salvation I helped you. Now is the day of salvation!" (2 Corinthians 6: 1)

Introduction by Jerome A. Henry

How exciting it would be to find that bottle and read the contents of the note contained inside. Now suppose the writer of the note was a President, a King or what if the message came from outside of our world, beyond time and space, wouldn't you be interested in reading it?

The fact is that we have a message just like that. The bible is a love letter from our Creator. What a treasure we have at our fingertips and what a tragedy if we never discover the wisdom contained inside. "All Scripture is given by inspiration of God, and is profitable for doctrine, for reproof, for correction, for instruction in righteousness, that the man of God may be complete, thoroughly equipped for every good work." 2 Timothy 3:16. NKJV

I talk to people who say they don't believe in God. They give me all sorts of reasons for their lack of faith but basically it comes down to the absence of solid evidence. Although misguided, they are in good company. Even one of Jesus' disciples, Thomas, said "Unless I see in His hands the print of the nails, and put my finger into the print of the nails, and put my hand into His side, I will not believe." John 20:25. NKJV

There are many infallible proofs for God's existence, all of which are found inside the pages of the bible. "So then faith comes by hearing, and hearing by the word of God." Romans 10:17 NKJV. But unless we open and hear the word, the seeds of faith can't be planted in our hearts. All faith takes is a seed, some water and some warm light from the Son.

Found near the end of the New Testament, is the book of Hebrews. Chapter eleven is called the "Hall of faith". There in verse 1 we find the definition of faith "Now faith is the substance of things hoped for, the evidence of things not seen." It's also said that without faith it's impossible to please God.

We're told Abel offered to God a more excellent sacrifice than Cain by offering up a lamb from the flock. God had instructed that our sin can only be covered up with blood. "And according to the law almost all things are purified with blood, and without the shedding of blood there is no remission of sin". Hebrews 9:22. NKJV

Noah who had never seen one drop of rain, by faith built an ark to God's specifications and saved his household of eight. The only people who did not perish in the worldwide deluge were the people who were safely on the ark. Once they were inside, it was God who shut the door and condemned the entire lost world outside.

On faith Abraham left his homeland and journeyed to a land he had never seen before. Even when God asked him to sacrifice his only son, Isaac, Abraham obeys and witnesses grace and mercy as God delivers Isaac from certain death by providing a ram caught in the thicket. Later on, it would happen that on that very same mountain, Moriah, God would provide His one and only son to become our sacrifice.

So God did send us a message but it was not hidden inside of a bottle. Instead, He carefully inspired men to record ahead of time foretelling what was going to happen in the future. Then through the blood of many martyrs, the books were canonized, published and distributed worldwide.

One day Jesus will return as the King of kings and the Lord of lords to shepherd His people and put an end to sin. At that time all of us who have put our trust in Him, will rejoice as the Lamb of God takes the scroll and breaks its seals, redeeming the earth.

"Therefore we also, since we are surrounded by so great a cloud of witnesses, let us lay aside every weight, and the sin which so easily ensnares us, and let us run with endurance the race that is set before us, looking unto Jesus, the author and finisher of our faith, who for the joy that was set before Him endured the cross, despising the shame, and has set down at the right hand of the throne of God." Hebrews 12:1, 2 NKJV

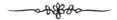

The perfect fit

I pushed on the heavy glass revolving doors and quickly stepped into the space created as they turned us slowly out into ninety degree Portland weather. Elise was patiently waiting curbside as my wife and I carried our carry-on bags atop our roller equipped suitcases.

The car was completely packed. My daughter had followed my instructions to the last detail. Everything had been neatly and perfectly packed into the Japanese commuter car I had asked her to rent for our trip.

"Please get an economy car, with a back-up camera that will get at least thirty-five to forty miles per gallon." I remembered saying to Elise, a week before our arrival, as she continued to beg for a slightly larger vehicle.

The traffic in the arrival area wasn't too bad today but the suitcases, my wife insisted we pack for our short five day trip, didn't want to fit into the trunk. While the cars continued to pile up behind us I continued to push until my wife's suitcase conceded, folding up into a space that was several times too small for it.

Sometimes, no most of the time, I tend to be a bit on the cheap side not thinking things through to their final conclusion or cost. Instead of making reservations at motels, like Elise had suggested, I decided that camping in Washington's State Park system would be a better choice chock full of family bonding experiences.

My grandson smiled at me from his car seat as I continued trying to stuff my backpack in on top of the ice chest that consumed all the space next to him. I had to push and compress it to get it in past the open door where upon arrival it immediately expanded to fill the entire space to the roof.

My wife was right again as she wagged her finger at me insisting, "You just do not think things through, next time I will be making all the reservations."

I chivalrously opened the sedan's front passenger door for her then humbly crammed myself into the space left over next to my grandson's car seat. It was a tight fit so I maneuvered a pillow in-between my left arm and his car seat.

"At least we have a back-up camera," I thought proudly to myself as Elise pressed the accelerator pedal to the floor and our adventure began to accelerate towards our final destination. "After all, it was only a five hour drive to Port Townsend, right?"

Sometimes our lives can resemble a car which has been crammed with so many things that we lose sight of our purpose and at times our destination. We aimlessly drive on not fully understanding what we were put on earth to accomplish. Relationships end up taking the backseat while allowing our circumstances to overwhelm us.

Remember that it is the people in our lives, the relationships that we make that should take the front seat as we travel though life. The baggage we carry with us will always be there, never having enough space or time to get it completely packed away. There are times, when we get ourselves into a tight place, where we need to use our back-up camera to get out of situations that so easily entangle us and consume our time.

Being part of another person's life, the relationships we have with them, are the only things that will be traveling with us as we take our final adventure into eternity. Our last road trip will come to an end as we arrive at our Father's house.

Upon our arrival there will not be a trailer packed full of material things traveling behind us. There will not be a list of things to do to consume our time; instead we will have the perfect fit into a community of faith filled people where this world's system will no longer dictate how we spend our time.

So don't be on the cheap side when it comes to relationships and divine appointments.

"But God, who is rich in mercy, because of His great love with which He loved us, even when we were dead in trespasses, made us alive together with Christ (by grace you have been saved), and raised us up together, and made us sit together in the heavenly places in Christ Jesus, that in the ages to come He might show the exceeding riches of His grace in His kindness toward us in Christ Jesus. For by grace you have been saved through faith, and that not of yourselves; it is the gift of God, not of works, lest anyone should boast. For we are His workmanship, created in Christ Jesus for good works, which God prepared beforehand that we should walk in them." Ephesians 2:4-10 NKJV.

A few of my favorite things

Sometimes I think the world could be fixed if we just had a roll of duct tape large enough. If we were marooned in the wilderness with only a bag containing duct tape, a roll of tie wire and self adhesive tape we could probably survive for years. Throw in a combination army knife along with a can of spray lubricant and we could, maybe, live comfortably for decades. Although these items would come in very handy, the only thing we really would need in that bag was a bible, the inspired word of God.

From the book of Genesis, where God explains how He created everything, to the book of Revelation, where God explains our future destiny, every single word and sentence has something for us to discover about the world in which we live. I'm very thankful God inspired these men to carefully record exactly what He wanted to say to us. So for this Thanksgiving, the first thing I am giving thanks for is the word of God.

I'm also thankful for bright, warm sunny days that never seem to want to end. They would be the kind of days that are filled with sweet aromas of roses, star jasmine and salty ocean air. The wind would be gently blowing my hair back out of my eyes just as the bow of my sail boat bounced off the crest of another rolling wave. A group of Pelicans would be gliding silently through the air maintaining a perfect chevron flight. For a moment, time would stand perfectly still and I find myself wishing I was eternally banished into this place, forever looking to the horizon in search of adventure.

As much as I like November's delightfully lazy afternoons, I would joyfully give them all up for a crisp December snow flurry. There is a moment right before it begins to snow where the air is so still; it's as if all of heaven's angels have just inhaled and are awaiting their cue to let the storehouses of snow open. It's quite wonderful to lie on the ground completely bundled up in all manner of wool; a scarf, sweater, mittens and sheepskin boots. Next comes the calming silence which completely envelopes you as lie there waiting and gazing up into the stormy gray sky. Then suddenly, out of nowhere you spot them, beautiful unique frozen flakes that gently swirl down and land on your eyelashes.

I'm also thankful for the end of the day when the boots come off and work disappears along with all my burdens, temporarily disappearing from my memory like yesterday's setting sun. The lights dim and take a back seat to a blazing warm fire that has been kindled in the living room wood stove just as the tea kettle begins to whistle. After pouring a cup of tea, I settle into my easy chair, grab my leather bound first addition of Sherlock Holms and quickly find myself transported into another time and place. I would be lost in distant folds of my imagination forever if it wasn't for the timer on the microwave rhythmically chiming, reminding me that I need to eat.

There is a long and winding road that leads to my house. It is a very pleasant drive and I find that it really relaxes me. I know I'm getting close to home when I leave the asphalt and wind my way up into the granite fortresses of Gaskill Peak. Usually, you can spot two hawks circling overhead and a black and white checkered peregrine falcon darting through my father's vineyard. Depending on the time of year, you might even catch a glimpse of a rattlesnake, fox or even a tarantula walking across the sandy road. All these creatures, both great and small, are my friends but it isn't until I'm opening my front door that I find what I'm truly thankful for.

So, what I am truly thankful for is my family. It's wonderful to have loved ones around to whom I can let my hair down and vent my frustrations. I'm thankful for my children too, even teenagers, who constantly remind me that I have allot yet to learn, and a wife who shares in all my joy, sorrow, pain, as well as my triumphs. Because without our friends and family, our houses would be empty and cold; there would be no one to share a hearth fire with or sing to and dance with.

So to everyone living in a warm, family filled home, I bid you a wonderful, happy Thanksgiving. But to all you who are alone, do not despair, grab your bible and find a local church which is opening their doors just for you, where you will find your Heavenly Father and many of His children there to greet you!

Water of Life

Life, it's everywhere. From the lowest depths of our great oceans to the outer limits of our atmosphere life is present, adapting and growing. As you examine the world around you water will be at the heart of this phenomenon. It's the requirement needed for all life to begin, grow and in which it flourishes. Even a tiny baby is protected and begins life surrounded by a watery bubble, safe and sound in their mother's womb.

In nature water is the only compound that can exist, on its own, in three phases (solid, liquid, gas) at the same time. Vast oceans of water cover our globe and surround the continents we live on becoming a giant buffering system for all life on earth. We watch and admire as water vapor is evaporated from these massive oceans rising into our atmosphere forming feather canyons and ice cream shaped cloud castles for our enjoyment. These heavy laden giants release their bounty of fresh water over land masses where the rain soaks the ground eventually flowing back into rivers and streams.

All you have to do is look through a microscope at a drop of pond water to discover it teaming with life. Our planet is an amazing incubator in which all life wants to thrive and compete for its place in the world. We marvel at their apparent connection to one another as well as their ability to adapt and survive in some extreme environmental conditions.

The realization that water is the essence of life has encouraged many cultures to incorporate water into their worship. They search far and wide, traveling up mighty rivers to their source hoping to find sacred springs or fountains of life that might preserve them in the hope of fighting off the inevitable aging process.

On a practical level there is nothing more satisfying to quench our thirst then a glass of water. Cool, clean, crystal clear water the essence of what your body needs to live by making up ninety plus percent of our body's mass. It is the quintessential element of all life.

Although we are mostly made of H_2O there is something more that makes us who we are. It's an elusive unique quality that makes Peter different from John or James. Although these traits can be acquired they also seem to be pre disposed at conception through our genes that are carefully recorded in our DNA.

Who we are, the way in which we see the world around us as well as interact with it transcends the physical world of molecules, elements and compounds. There's an elusive spark to life that is hard to put our finger on, which can't be ignored and is present in all living things to one degree or another.

This breath of life that fills us and animates us is responsible for turning ordinary inorganic dust into living breathing creatures. We are totally helpless at birth but created with an innate ability to make a sound so nerve racking that our parents would be motivated to attend to our every need. There is also a genetic-parental-emotional connection that insures that our parents will provide, protect and nurture us.

Our Creator has designed into us and the life around us amazing systems to ensure our survival. He was the One, who in the very beginning filled lifeless earth with His own breath thus turning dust into living creatures. "So God created man in His own image; in the image of God He created them; male and female He created them." Genesis 1:27 NKJV

Jesus taught that all creation needed to do was cry out to their Heavenly Father and he would provide what they needed "Ask, and it will be given you; seek, and you will find; knock, and it will be opened to you. For everyone who asks receives, and he who seeks finds, and to him who knocks it will be opened." Matthew 7:7 NKJV

Jesus went on to explain that if we as ordinary parents only give good gifts to our own children when they ask, then how much more will our Heavenly Father give to those who ask of Him!

God loves us. He had a plan in place from the very beginning and that plan is still on schedule, and by the way it's His schedule. What an incredible world we live in that is filled with wonder at every turn. Are you ready to exercise your free will by calling out to your Heavenly Father?

In the last chapter, of the last book in the bible there is an invitation to all creation. "And the Spirit and the bride say, Come! And let him who hears say, Come! And let him who thirsts come. Whoever desires, let him take the water of life freely." Revelation 22:17 NKJV

Jesus is the water of life!

The wind under my wings

Cars were passing me as if I was a picket fence. I usually don't have a problem going the speed limit usually the reverse is true but today I was preoccupied with texting. So first off, I want you to know that I was not physically texting while driving but instead using my smart phone's "hands off" auto dictation option. It is actually refreshing, liberating and excellent use of my time to have both hands on the steering wheel, my eyes on the road and communicating.

When I got to bible study Donny was busy cleaning up the Youth Center. You can imagine after 8 hours of use how much of a mess thirty-five children can make.

"Hey pastor, what's cooking?" asks Donny with a smile as he maneuvered his motorized wheelchair to take a trash bag out to the dumpster in the parking lot. You see Donny is a volunteer and a soldier in Christ's army. He is always available to pray with people while hitching a ride on the bus or while holding up a cardboard sign that says "God loves you!" Suddenly while watching Donny I felt humbled and reflected on how often I start complaining about things.

So feeling a little guilty for the way in which I let myself be overwhelmed with daily life I turned and asked Donny "What keeps you going, where does your strength come from and what is your favorite verse you like to reflect on?"

"Well pastor, there is work to be done, Jesus Christ keeps me going and I love to read Psalm 61" smiled Donny.

Its dark after the study as Donny says goodbye and begins a journey of seven miles on the highway in his wheel chair back home. I began to think to myself "Man what a whiner I am". So on my way home after completing a couple more "hands free" texts, I push the button on my phone and say "Genie, I love you" to which the female voice on my phone responds "You are the wind under my wings", by the way if you know my wife please don't tell her I talk to my phone that way.

"Hear my cry, O God; Attend to my prayer. From the end of the earth I will cry to you, when my heart is overwhelmed; lead me to the rock that is higher than I. For you have been a shelter for me, a strong tower from the enemy. I will abide in your tabernacle forever; I will trust in the shelter of your wings. For you, O God, have heard my vows; you have given me the heritage of those who fear your name. You will prolong the king's life, his years as many generations. He shall abide before God forever. Oh, prepare mercy and truth, which may preserve him! So I will sing praise to your name forever, that I may daily perform my vows." Psalm 61 NKJV

I wonder if God looks at us in the same way Genie answered me "You are the wind under my wings"? What a word picture that is for God's love where we fill the space under his wings; that we were created for that very reason. He values and loves us so much that He gave His One and Only Son for us; and yet while we were sinners, Jesus Christ was born into this world to save it. It's so good to know and better to believe that God's wings are a shelter from the storms in this life.

Because when Donny's heart is overwhelmed he goes to God's word for comfort and through the shelter of His wings, through the power of the Holy Spirit, the Father will lead him back to the Rock that is higher than I. Even in our own lives when problems arise and our enemies lie in wait, again God is a strong tower that we can run into. The tent or tabernacle of His presence will be incredibly sufficient to deliver us through the veil of death and usher us into His presence. So tell me, what is there that we should fear?

King David, who wrote this psalm as his son Absalom is forcefully taking over his kingdom throwing him out of Jerusalem into the wilderness, must have felt abandoned and forsaken by God. So even though David felt like he was at the ends of the earth God was always there with him, listening to his prayers, preparing him to get back out there and engage the enemy.

So I'm indebted to Donny who by his trust in God has showed me not to fear when the battle begins to heat up but to run to the Rock that is higher than I!

Washing feet

One by one the apostles walked through the doorway into the upper room that had been prepared for the Passover. As each guest passed through the opening, they noticed a pitcher full of water, a bowl to pour it into as well as a towel to wipe the dirt from their feet but where was the servant?

The first one to arrive at the empty doorway was Peter. He was puzzled why the owner had neglected to station someone there to wash their feet and began to yell for some help but nobody answered his call. Frustrated he flipped his sandals from his feet; they hit the wall with a loud thud knocking mud off onto the newly swept floor. John was following close behind and carrying the lamb which was to be prepared for the celebration supper. Peter turned towards John, thinking for a minute that he should take the towel and wash John's feet. However, the thought quickly evaporated. For weeks now Peter, John, James and the other nine disciples had been arguing about who was considered to be the greatest one among them.

As John crossed the threshold, he noticed how dirty his feet were and before stepping any further called out in a loud voice for the house servant but there was no answer. With a lamb in his arms, he couldn't really bend down to wash his own feet, so for a moment he glanced over at Peter who was busy preparing the herbs in a bowl on a low lying table located in the back. John bit his lip and started to say "Pe_t_er" but the syllables just spilled out as unrecognizable sounds in his throat.

Next, James thoughtlessly burst right into the upper room completely forgetting that his sandals were caked with mud mixed with donkey manure. He was in such a hurry that he had carelessly step in a fresh pile down near the entrance where a foal was tied up. Peter turning towards the door saw the mess on the floor and quickly scolded James then went back to work secretly thinking about how much of a hypocrite he was. James quickly put the flask of wine down onto the table along with a small pouch of sea salt. He frantically tried to clean his own feet but ended up adding to the mess that was already on the floor.

Soon the rest of the apostles would be coming up the steps that led to the upper room. "Clunk, clunk, clunk" pounded the sandals on stair treads as Andrew, Philip and Bartholomew came to an abrupt stop and waited for someone to wash their feet. They looked around for anyone but there wasn't a soul around to help. Peter, John and James were all busy preparing a part of the feast and as elders in their group, they were above such menial tasks.

Soon the other James appeared followed by Matthew, Thomas, Thaddeus, Simon and Judas who all entered one by one. Quickly and silently they sat down reclining at the table carefully hiding their unwashed feet under the table. These men had been arguing since they had left Galilee about who was the greatest among them so that nobody was about to volunteer to wash the other's feet. Nobody wanted to stoop to do the lowest job in the house. It was at that point that Jesus entered the room.

"With fervent desire I have desired to eat this Passover with you before I suffer; for I say to you, I will no longer eat of it until it is fulfilled in the kingdom of God." Jesus, knowing that the Father had given all things into His hands, and that He had come from God and was going to God, rose from supper and laid aside His garments, took a towel and girded Himself. After that, He poured water into a basin and began to wash the disciples' feet, and to wipe them with the towel with which He was girded." Luke 22:14-16 and John 13:3-5 NKJV

Oh, how we all need to be washed by the Master. God loved us so much that He willingly left heaven and became a man to die in our place. There is no greater love than that where a man willingly lays down his life for a friend. Jesus Christ allowed His own creation to falsely accuse Him, mock and beat Him and executed on a cross.

What an incredible scene it must have been that night in the upper room as Jesus gently washed the dirt off of all their feet. At that moment It might have been only the dirt acquired that day but as soon as Jesus died He washed away all of our sins. So who is this King of Glory? His name is Jesus!

Blue

How would you go about describing what the color blue looks like to a sightless person? Someone who was blind from birth would be unable to understand what blue was. If you were incredibly clever you might get a pan from the kitchen fill it with ice and water and then put the blind person's hand into the cold mixture. This might convey certain aspects of things that might be blue in color but it would not be the complete visual package. Bottom line, you still won't know what the color blue looks like.

We actually live in a universe where we can interpret four dimensions. Let's start by saying we exist as one point in infinite space. Now let's add another point to our universe and now we arrive at our first dimension which is "length". One more point added to the mix and suddenly we have our second dimension which is "width". Our next dimension is "height" which gives us our X, Y and Z axis or our three dimensional universe. The last known dimension is "time". What really is time?

To have "time" in our universe we need to have matter and it needs to be set into motion. If objects are not moving then there is nothing to measure because you have to have time in order to travel distance. If we stood perfectly still somewhere in space and nothing was in motion, we would not feel the passage of time. Also, without motion, we would not have light waves or light particles so wondering what the color blue looked like would be a moot issue. It really would be mute because we would not have sound waves either.

Now let's think back to being blind or sightless and wanting to discover the truth about the color blue. What story would you attempt to tell someone to describe the color blue? What props could you use to convey the color blue? Just think about this dilemma. How to pass information from one known dimension to another unknown dimension? This is what I refer to as an extra-dimensional information transmission dilemma.

Do you believe in a literal place the bible calls Hell? Jesus did and he spent a lot of time warning us about the dangers of ending up there. Although where it is and what it really is seems a little bit like describing the color blue to a sightless person. Some of the biblical descriptions of hell include a place where the worm never dies, the lake of fire, a lake burning with fire and brimstone, a place of wailing and gnashing of teeth,

We are given a word picture of an extra dimensional reality that we cannot yet comprehend because I believe it literally exits in another dimension. Jesus was warning us of a situation so terrible, so wicked that the only reference point He had here on earth was the Jerusalem trash dump located in the valley of Hinnom (Gehenna). This place not only smelled bad, it was always burning with smoke and flame that continually filled the sky. This horrible stench would probably drift into the city and remind people of the dump and all the discarded trash as the wind blew it into town. In older times, child sacrifice to Molech also took place in this area.

What word picture, from here on earth, would come close to describing such an awesome place? Think about the blind person's hand in the ice water in an attempt to describe the color blue. How would you describe a place void of God's love? Hell is a real place that is void of God's love, His light, His warmth and His fellowship. No wonder Jesus was warning us not to choose that place.

Choose Jesus now, God has gone through much pain and suffering to keep us out of hell! Jesus is the "Way" to God. He has said this about Himself; He is the beginning and the end, He was the one who was alive and was dead and is alive for evermore, He alone holds the keys to death and Hades.

"The wicked shall be turned into hell, And all the nations that forget God. For the needy shall not always be forgotten; The expectation of the poor shall not perish forever. Arise, O Lord Do not let man prevail; Let the nations be judged in your sight. Put them in fear, O Lord That the nations may know themselves to be but men." psalm 9:17-20 NKJV

Jesus invites you to come just as you are. The Holy Spirit will draw and seal you, while the cross reminds us of what it cost God to escape the horrors of hell. You don't have to go there to believe it exists.

About time

It's been said before that there is a time for everything. If only I had enough time to do everything, enough steps ordained in my life to see all the things I wanted to see in the entire world. As it is, I barley have enough time to see all of the country where I live. It still amazes me every time I turn down a road I have never traveled on.

Truthfully, I'm jealous of people who have time to travel the world. I watch with wonder as some sail the world's oceans, trek through high and lofty mountains while still others explore metropolitan areas that are buzzing with people infused in art and entertainment.

I'm also mystified at how so many people can spend so much of their time reading books. They take every available spare moment to get through another couple of pages where they get lost in some mystery, adventure or romance. I'm puzzled by people who also spend hours trying to figure out crossword, jigsaw and accounting problems.

On the other side of the coin people can do exhilarating things that defy our imagination. Astronauts have traveled vast distances through time to walk and perform research on the moon. Accomplished artists as well as composers have withstood the test of time while other's art is not discovered until after their untimely passing.

At my dermatologist's office there is a picture on the wall of my doctor with her arms around a 8oo pound male tiger. Another friend of mine has a picture of himself falling through the atmosphere with seven other skydivers linked together in the shape of a star. For the record, even if I had enough time to hug a tiger or jump out of an airplane I still wouldn't do either of those things.

In my opinion the hobbits that exist between the pages of J.R. Tolkien's books have mastered the correct way to saddle the passage of time. Through many ages they have perfected the cultivation of lush gardens, mastered the cultivation of Old Toby and fermented the world's greatest ale.

So why I'm I spending so much time on this subject and where is it leading us?

The world, like any great symphony, is heading for a crescendo. The music will heard around the globe while the main movement will be focused on the city of Jerusalem, Israel. We can actually pinpoint the location in Israel's capitol, a hill known in earlier times as Mount Moriah. It's a special piece of real estate to God; it's near the place where Jesus was crucified and where what's left of the Jewish Temple Complex lies in rubble waiting to be re-built for the third and last time The world stage is now being set as we speak and the final curtain is being drawn open.

In Judaism, the question of ownership of the Temple Mount has never been questioned by serious bible scholars and world historians. The construction and existence of several Islamic buildings (mosques), on land purchased by Israel's King David on the ancient Jewish Temple Mount, is a fairly recent event when viewed on a time line of world history.

President Donald Trump, just recently, has taken a bold resounding step to recognize Jerusalem as the capital of Israel by beginning to move the United States embassy from Tel Aviv to Jerusalem. Although there will be much debate and dispute over this situation there can be no question as to who actually owns the Temple Mount.

In the Old Testament book of 2 Samuel, recorded in the tenth century BC, the author records a sales transaction between King David and Araunah for the purchase of the area known as the Temple Mount.

"Then the king said to Araunah, 'No but I will surely buy it from you for a price; nor will I offer burnt offerings to the Lord my God with that which costs me nothing.' So David bought the threshing floor and the oxen for fifty shekels of silver." 2 Samuel 24:21-25 NKJV

The Islamic mosques that stand on the site, near where the first and second Jewish Temples once stood, were built some 1700 years later, after King David purchased the real estate for the nation of Israel. In the Old Testament book of Ezekiel God promises that in the end times His Temple will be re-built for the third and last time.

For all Christians our bodies have become the Temple of the Holy Spirit. The Helper, who now resides in us, is waiting for the right time when the Bridegroom will return to the earth to receive His bride to Himself. Have you made the decision to follow Jesus before time runs out and the last blast of the trumpet is heard around the world?

A moment in time

Can you remember a single moment in your life that you wished would never end? You might have been with your best friend, a spouse or maybe you were alone somewhere but where ever it was you did not want time to stop. I have had several moments in my life where the sun seemed to stand still and the universal clock stopped ticking. In this euphoria, while basking in the warmth of the sun, I have experienced real peace. It was as if time no longer existed and that the sun in all of its glory just stopped and stood still in the center of the sky offering me a second of eternity.

Can you describe a place you have never been to? An island perhaps complete with coarse coral sand crunching under your feet or a warm tropical breeze as it moves palm fronds around. Theologians have had trouble describing this concept about the afterlife or heaven to others in a meaningful way. The apostle John tried to describe a vision of heaven to us as he described heavenly things in the book of Revelation 5:6-10. For me I have reasoned in my own mind that there is another place after this physical life passes away. I believe certain euphoric feelings we have in this life, where we wish a single moment will never end, is what we will experience when we pass on into the presence of God.

My wife and I love to watch movies about time travel where time seems to be more accessible and fluid than how we think of it now, as being more ridged and fixed. Now, I can't remember anything before I was born except a very early memory of being on a large island surrounded by water, wet sand beneath my feet and a cool breeze blowing through my hair. Do you dream about a similar place or nexus, a place outside this dimension where we will live in the presence of an almighty, all loving God? The bible teaches us that when we finally arrive there we won't need the sun to stand still that the glory of God provides all the light we will need!

So as Joshua needs more daylight to complete the great slaughter of their enemies he prays for the sun to be halted in its path and the moon to stop where it stood (Joshua 10:12-15). Now for us reading these passages today about 1200 to 1350 years before Christ was born, it seems surrealistic to think that God would not only approve the slaughter of every man, woman and child but He orchestrated it. Then ponder the thought about the earth having to stop revolving for the sun and moon to stand still and you quickly get into the realm of faith. Can any of us call fire down from heaven, demolish fortresses with horns blowing or stop the earth from turning?

All of us if we had that kind of power would wield it against our brothers and sisters without giving it a second thought to the consequences. But on the other hand If we look at Jesus, who had the power to do all these things and more, how He lived and loved and how many people hated Him to the point of wanting to kill Him. They despised and plotted against Him, the God that created them, who created everything we see around us, allowed Himself to be led like a lamb to the slaughter. Greater love has no man that would lay down his life for his friends. Jesus went willingly to His crucifixion, suffering a grueling, barbaric and slow death on a Roman torture device.

"And I looked, and behold, in the midst of the throne and of the four living creatures, and in the midst of the elders, stood a Lamb as though it had been slain, having seven horns and seven eyes, which are the seven Spirits of God sent out into all the earth. Then He came and took the scroll out of the right hand of Him who sat on the throne. Now when He had taken the scroll, the four living creatures and the twenty-four elders fell down before the Lamb, each having a harp, and golden bowls full of incense, which are the prayers of the saints. And they sang a new song, saying: "'You are worthy to take the scroll, And to open its seals; For You were slain, And have redeemed us to God by Your blood Out of every tribe and tongue and people and nation, And have made us kings and priests to our God; And we shall reign on the earth.'" Revelation 5:6-10 NKJV.

A.R.K. Acts of random kindness

The alarm hadn't gone off yet but I got up anyway and blindly walked down the hallway towards the kitchen. In the early morning darkness I managed to step on my kitten's tail, bump into some pictures hanging on the wall and catch my little toe on the edge of a door. After pouring some water, grinding coffee beans and a couple colorful metaphors I readied my worn-out coffee pot for its daily duty.

While standing alone in the darkness waiting for the water to boil I noticed a shopping list on the kitchen island. The neatly scratched note in my wife's handwriting read "12-bags, 12-water, 4-tissue, 6-toothbrush, 5-sanitizer, 12-hats, 12-gloves, 12- socks, hard candy, $5.00 bills, shampoo, lip balm, sun screen, deodorant and something else I couldn't make out what it was.

For a moment I thought she was preparing to run away but with $5.00 bills? Wouldn't she need something larger for traveling money and why would she need twelve hats and twelve pairs of gloves? For several minutes the mystery bounced off and around inside my nearly empty cranial cavity before making the connection somewhere in the deep recesses of my brain.

Then it dawned on me that my wife was preparing to hand out emergency care packages to help homeless men, women and children. (I'll have to warn her to watch herself around some parks and other city owned property where recent emergency ordinances make it a crime to help the less fortunate.)

The last time I handed out these bags for my wife I was concerned that I wouldn't be able to find anyone to give them to. But after parking my car off Fourth Avenue I barely made it three blocks before all the bags were gone. I think it's the $ 5.00 bill that catches their initial attention and puts a smile on their grateful faces.

So right now I can hear all you critics saying "You shouldn't give homeless people money! They will buy drugs and alcohol with it!" Great so let's not do anything to help the less fortunate because we don't want them to make bad decisions. Have you ever made any bad decisions?

This Christmas season we have a choice to give away our love or to be misers and hold onto every last penny like Ebenezer Scrooge. The choice is always yours but from my experience when you choose to bless someone else it always seems to happen that you are the one who gets the blessing in the end.

It's so thrilling to drive around my town and see so many of you are now in full swing putting up colorful lights and other decorations around your house to celebrate the birth of the Christ Child. Wouldn't it be wonderful if all of our town's churches started putting up nativity scenes depicting Mary, Joseph, shepherds, animals and of course the baby Jesus? The ones with the three magi are cool too but in all actuality they didn't come to worship the Lord until at least a year or two later.

Now as we have two weeks left to focus our attention on shopping for Christmas presents let us not forget the truly needy, hungry or homeless in our communities. I'm not talking about the professional panhandlers who hold up cardboard signs while flashing fancy watches, nice clothes or a large cafe cup.

Also after leaving the grocery store or department stores listen for the bell ringer and look for the red kettle to slip a ten or twenty dollar bill into. These organizations are not fleecing the flock but putting your contribution to good work clothing, feeding and sheltering the homeless.

Random acts of kindness always make you feel good. Also pray for parking spaces and not prey on them as you're out searching for last minute gifts. Support our towns commerce too by shopping locally. There are many clothing stores, bike shops, gun shops, massage therapists, flower stores and many other merchants we can support right here in our home town.

So as all the consumerism, tinsel and flocking continues let us not forget the real reason we are celebrating this special season. God gave His One and only Son as a gift to save the world from sin.

"For unto us a Child is born, unto us a Son is given; and the government will be upon His shoulder. And His name will be called Wonderful, Counselor, Mighty God, Everlasting Father, Prince of Peace. Of the increase of His government and peace there will be no end, upon the throne of David and over His kingdom, to order it and establish it with judgment and justice from that time forward, even forever." Isaiah 9:6-7 NKJV.

Deep waters

Donny carefully slid out of the kayak and into the deep blue waters of the pacific. The water was cool at first but soon warmed as he dipped his mask into the water for a look at the reef. Donny and Jane had paddled over to the north end of Kealakekua Bay just to the left of the white monument that had been constructed to remember the spot where Captain Cook was murdered.

The current was extremely swift just outside of the rocky point where Donny wanted to dive. The waves, crashing against the rocks around them, added to Jane's anxiety as the two stared down into deep blue waters. A large school of black sail fish schooled around Donny and Jane as they surveyed their new surroundings. The terraced coral reef was colorful, beautiful and teaming with all varieties of colorful fish which darted and ducted into holes in the reef as the couple kicked their way towards the point.

Looking straight down the nearly vertical slope of the reef Donny strained his eyes to see down as the clear blue waters slowly faded into an eerie black abyss. In the distance a massive Manta ray sailed through the water nearly brushing up against the couple as it eventually disappeared back into deep waters of the vast Pacific Ocean from where it came.

Jane turned her attention back to life on the reef marveling at the amount of diversity as a variety of fish darted in and out of the coral. Other creatures clung to the reef or stayed in large schools for their own protection from the larger fish that inhabited the shadows of the deep waters below their complex reef community.

Donny took in several deep breaths and attempted to dive straight down into the blackness that hung like a black velvet veil below him. Down he went ten; twenty, thirty feet finally maxing out at 45 feet as the colder water stopped him from going deeper. Still something seemed to be calling out luring him on towards the phantom bottom that lurked below.

In life just as in our ocean reef community, we often find ourselves in deep waters. Sometimes it's just the ordinary pressures of life and other times the surge increases as we find ourselves in the midst of a tempest.

Just as in the case of our ocean community we too need each other and can find safety and solace as we gather together in community. Jesus hinted at this when He said "For where two or three are gathered together in My name, I am there in the midst of them."

We were never meant to walk through life alone. God designed us in such a way that we would not only desire a relationship with Him but also need fellowship with each other. We need fellowship, true fellowship where we are lift up each other as we swim through the often-fast currents of life.

God's love is like very deep waters where there is no end to the depths of His love. Many times, we often are too scared to venture into those deep waters as we cling to the security of reef life. However, if we do let go and venture out into the deeper water then we have a chance to see how magnificent His love, mercy and grace really is.

Life is full of many dangers, toils and snares; some lead to death but if we let go and dive into the deep love of God we will never be afraid as He promises to guide us into safe harbor. He is the One who fills our sails with wind moving us over the sometimes rough waters of the ocean then as our spiritual sails fill with His Holy Spirit we are now safely on course for our eternal destination.

God loves us. He isn't angry with us but instead is deeply concerned about us when we veer off course or run aground on the hidden, submerged reefs of life. His hands are always open to help and all we have to do is call out to Him and He will hear our voices. No matter how lost we might feel, no matter how alone we might be, God is always there. He is a Father to the fatherless and His love is pure, good and holy.

Walking with God, trusting God is the best adventure we can ever set out on. As we see His hand on our life and feel the Holy Spirit's influence in our lives we will begin to swim away from the shallow reefs and begin to explore the deeper waters of a life and relationship surround by the depths of His love.

Divine watchmaker

Let's think about the task of producing a working watch for a moment. Our first step would require planning, design and blueprints. Only then could we design and create the machines be to forge and produce each individual part needed to assemble a watch. All of the miniature springs, gears and movements will have to be designed and built to extreme tolerances. Now supposing we take all these brand new parts and throw them out into a field. How many millions of years of evolution would go by before they accidentally assemble themselves into a functional watch?

Creationists believe that our universe had a beginning and will also have an end. They admit to seeing inescapable elements of design in the sub-atomic world, in our own world and the entire universe in which we live. There are too many aspects of design literally all around us. Obvious evidence that the watch maker was not blind but indeed can see beyond the physical limits of time and space! The following story is an example of how God inspired 40 different authors to write 66 books over a period of 2,000 years and still manage to maintain literary consistency.

When I was about 15 years old I began a search for the truth. I remember my search eventually landed me at the foot of the cross. I went forward to receive Christ, making a public confession of faith, at the altar of a worship service at my local church. I began to study the bible only to be frustrated with such a large book filled with names I couldn't pronounce, places I've never heard of and stories I did not understand. One example is found in the gospel of John 3:1-21.

In this story Jesus is talking to a Pharisee named Nicodemus. He has come to Jesus by night, under the cover of darkness to hide his identity, to hear from Him what God wanted to say to mankind. Jesus tells him that unless one is born again he cannot see the kingdom of God. To which Nicodemus responds "How can a man be born when he is old? Can he enter a second time into his mother's womb and be born?"

Jesus explains that a man must first be born into the physical world through the flesh then born into the spiritual world through the Spirit in order to see the kingdom of God. In John 3:14 Jesus uses an Old Testament prophecy hidden within the writings of Moses to illuminate the answer for Nicodemus.

"And as Moses lifted up the serpent in the wilderness, even so must the Son of Man be lifted up; that whoever believes in Him should not perish but have eternal life."

Now if you are a new believer or someone who has not studied the Old Testament this quote from Jesus will make absolutely no sense. On the other hand if you have taken the time to study this story in Numbers 21:9, which was written by Moses 1500 years before the birth of Jesus of Nazareth, you will see evidence showing that God inspired this prophecy to point to a future moment in time.

The children of Israel had been wandering around in the desert grumbling and complaining. So the Lord sent fiery serpents that bit the people and many died. The people repented and asked Moses to pray for God's intervention. God instructs Moses to make a fiery serpent and place it on a pole and when someone was bitten if they looked up to the serpent on the pole they lived.

It's both interesting and at the same time very odd that God instructed Moses to make a bronze serpent and had him place it on a pole to be lifted up. The serpent represented the original sin from the Garden of Eden while the bronze it was made from represented judgment, so together it was symbolic of "sin judged".

Now 1500 years later Jesus is making reference to this Old Testament story at the same time as Nicodemus is asking basically "How a man must be saved?" Jesus is pointing out to him and all of us that in a few short days He Himself would be nailed to a wooden pole then lifted up to die for the sins of the world; and as many who would choose to look up to Him, believe in Him would be saved!

Our Devine watchmaker even inspired His-story to be written in advance so that in hearing we might believe in the provision of His Son. All who confess with their mouth and believe in their heart that God raised Jesus from the dead is saved!

Washed clean

Cornelius was a gentile Centurion, of the Italian regiment, living Caesarea who feared and believed in the one true and living God of Abraham, Isaac and Jacob. Peter was a Jewish fisherman by trade, living in Jerusalem, who was now following Jesus of Nazareth the son of man and the only begotten Son of God. They were both in the mind of God as our Heavenly Father begins to orchestrate a divine appointment that would unite, essentially graft in, a non Jewish world into the newly formed church of Jesus Christ.

In a vision an angel of God tells Cornelius to seek out Simon Peter who was staying with a friend in the Mediterranean port village of Joppa. At the same time, several miles away, Peter is praying on a rooftop as God sends him a vision of a great sheet being lowered down from heaven by its four corners. In it were all the forbidden foods that God had told the nation of Israel not to eat. Peter is instructed that God has now cleansed these things and for him to partake in them.

"But peter said, "Not so Lord! For I have never eaten anything common or unclean" and a voice spoke to him a second time, "What God has cleansed you must not call common." Acts 10:14,15 NKJV. While Peter is thinking about the meaning of this vision the three men Cornelius sent to get him arrive at his lodgings. The Spirit says to Peter "Behold three men are seeking you. Arise, therefore, go down and go with them, doubting nothing; for I have sent them." Acts 10:19-20 NKJV.

When Peter arrives in the compound of Cornelius there is a very large crowd of family and friends who have gathered to hear the truth of God explained by this Jewish preacher. "In truth I perceive that God shows no partiality. But in every nation who fears Him and works righteousness is accepted by Him. The word which God sent to the children of Israel, preaching peace through Jesus Christ- He is Lord of all."

What God has cleansed let no man call common! God shows no partiality, no matter where you're from Europe, South America, Africa, Pacific Islands or Asia; He loves every single person He has created. I know it must have been hard, almost impossible for the nation of Israel to understand that God had cleansed all men and that they were now being invited into His kingdom but that was exactly what He had done.

For the truth is we have all sinned and fallen short of the glory of God and one of the biggest areas we come up short is religion. It's interesting that even though God solved our sin problem, by sending His only Son into the world to pay a debt we could never pay, men over the centuries have insisted that there has to be more work involved. However, salvation is a gift from God.

Many religious systems and Christian denominations believe that their way of achieving salvation is the only way and that you must be a member of their organization to obtain it. Rubbish! God left Moses standing on the edge of the Promised Land, unable to enter, because of His unbelief that God Himself is the only way to receive salvation. Laws, rules and regulations will never deliver you into the hands of a Living God. It was Joshua who led the nation of Israel into the Promise Land and who was a fore shadow of Jesus Christ who is both the author and finisher of our salvation.

The day that Jesus Christ died was the day that all of mankind was completely forgiven; what God has cleansed let no man call common or unclean. This is the gospel and it really is that simple so don't complicate things. Jesus Himself said that the truth would set us free from the law of sin and bondage. There is only one God, only one Savior who has broken down the walls of separation.

So logically there can only be one church, one living organism that is being created and built by God, where Jesus Christ is the everlasting King! God loves His world and His desire is that all men come to Him through His Son, Jesus Christ.

So if you find yourself sitting in a building on Saturday, Sunday or any day or night of the week where a man or woman is insisting that there is more to your salvation then get up out of your seat and run for the exit! For there is a new everlasting kingdom approaching whose King shall be called Wonderful, Counselor, Mighty God, Everlasting Father and the Prince of Peace. For what God has cleansed, let no man call unclean!

The empty stairwell

I know of this church in the city where there is an enclosed stairwell in which the homeless go in search of safety and shelter. A couple of weeks ago I discovered a couple pairs of feet sticking out of the stairwell. I didn't want to wake the individuals who were attached to the feet so I went to the church's copy room which doubles as my office and sitting down began to read my bible.

No sooner had I read through the first sentence God spoke to my heart as clear as can be and said "Make them breakfast". I thought about it for awhile then quickly went to work in the kitchen fixing up a couple plates of food. Nothing too fancy just some scrambled eggs, cut up hot dogs and a bun wrapped in tin foil and carried with love out to the stairwell.

When I appeared back out at the stairwell I must have startled the young man and woman who were fast asleep. They did not want any trouble and were very eager to leave without incident.

"We don't want any trouble; we will leave" said the young man.

"Wait" I said with a smile "I made you breakfast".

Their eyes widened and both of their jaws dropped. They were hungry and also needed to use the church's restrooms. When they returned I was able to share my faith in Jesus Christ. Remember, People don't care how much you know until they know how much you care. Actions speak louder than words.

Eddie and Joanna were Native American Indians from the Rincon tribe. Eddie was 20 years old while Joanna, I later found out later, was 24 years old. Eddie had just been released from jail on a petty theft charge, caught shoplifting food from a mini mart. He was trying to feed his family.

The stairwell has been used by many street travelers over the years as a safe haven for the night. These kids were no exception. They had nowhere to go. I have been homeless myself before so I can totally relate to their situation. I had no problem with the couple seeking refuge in the stairwell but as it turned out the rest of the church did.

"It's against the law" said one church staffer.

"We were told by the police not to let people sleep on our property." said another associate pastor.

"Please don't encourage them to sleep here" said someone else.

"I had to paint the stairwell 2 times last week because they really messed it up" said one of the maintenance workers. So the decision was made and signs went up in the stairwell "No sleeping allowed in the stairwell".

This is where my heart broke. These could be my own children. Jesus taught us to help others. Why do people hold material things higher than real people? Why was it so hard just to help these kids the best we can? Wouldn't it be simpler just continuing to clean up the stairwell?

Dawn came early today as I arrived to do my usual cleaning of the church before everyone began arriving. As I passed the empty stairwell, all bright and clean with a brand new coat of paint, I remembered Eddie and Joanna and the expression on their faces as they ate their breakfast. I wondered if the right decision was made. I know an opportunity to love two souls, in Jesus name, was missed. So the last few nights passed without the restlessness of

Eddie and Joanna constant turning in an attempt to find a comfortable spot on the cold concrete of the landing.

Well I know where there is a cold, empty stairwell on the boulevard tonight. It's a lonely stairwell that once kept two young souls safe from the dangers of a night on the street. It is now however a very clean, bright and shiny place complete with a fresh coat of gray paint, you might even call its appearance pristine. But I liked it better dirty, urine soaked with cigarette ashes caught in the corners of the landing where it stood as a standing reminder that there are people in need of our help. I liked the stairwell better when it had two pairs of warm human feet sticking out.

I wonder which stairwell Jesus Christ would have preferred. I ponder the thought as to whether the people in our church would have allowed Him to sleep there? Material things will be left behind but the relationships we make will last for eternity.

The bench

The bench sat alongside a lonely stretch of dirt road under the shadow of Gaskill Peak. Day after day horse drawn wagons passed by but their riders never bothered to stop and enjoy the breathtaking views from the bench. Many full moons passed when a woman appeared planting flowers around the wooden bench. Soon the bulbs sprouted and grew into beautiful spring lilies that seem to clothe the bench in a beautiful God-spun coat of many colors. The woman also placed a small twisted circle of woven briers complete with large thorns over a rusty spike that had been driven into an old rugged wooden cross which stood behind and to the left of the bench.

Soon spring left the bench to be pummeled by the scorching winds of summer. As the last drops of moisture from the bench's wooden slats evaporated into thin air, the bench began to crack and split. When cooler nights came the bench would gaze up at the stars wondering if this was all there was to life? He knew he had a purpose in life but still nobody ever seemed to find time to sit and enjoy his comfort and majestic views of the surrounding hills.

One day, as a gentle breeze began blowing, several leaves floated down from the heights coming to rest on the seat of the bench. The leaves startled but delighted the bench all dressed in their brightly colored warm hues of red, orange and yellow. The woman who planted the spring flowers and hung the crown of thorns returned to pay the bench a visit. She was not alone and in her arms was a black cloaked figure which was holding a pumpkin. The pumpkin had been carved with a face and a flickering candle illuminated its interior.

One evening, as a full moon crested over the hills, the bench had many unexpected visitors. Hordes of children came by to stare at the ghoulish figure that was unmoved. The kids were all dressed up in costumes complete with scary masks that covered their faces. They all stopped to stare at the mysterious figure sitting on the bench who was holding his pumpkin head in his hands. They all laughed and giggled and some boys even threw rocks at the headless ghost's glowing head. The bench was overjoyed that someone was actually taking notice of him and had hardly noticed the rocks that the little boys had bounced off his back.

Soon clouds began to gather pushing themselves up against the tall mountain sides. The gathering gloom brought with it rain and sleet that covered the ground. One night, as the temperature began to drop, the sleet turned into beautiful flakes of snow. Each flake was unique as it swirled through the cold night air landing so very lightly on the top of the bench's seat. The swirling night air caused a shiver to move down his back. During the day, wagons carrying the harvest in from the fields made ruts in the muddy dirt road. The wagons were overflowing with corn, pumpkins, gourds and all sorts of fruit and vegetables. There were so many things to be thankful for, but still nobody came by to visit him. The woman who been there so many times before hadn't been by in a long time he began to worry that she might not come back.

As the storms continued pounding the countryside, the snow began to pile up around the bench until one day he couldn't see anything at all. He sat for many days and nights alone shivering in the solitude of a snow drift. Then one day he heard someone shoveling snow and the familiar voice of the woman. She was singing hymns with each scoop of the shovel as the cold wet snow was removed.

At last the warmth of the sun was beginning to shine on Him. The woman began adorning him with brightly colored glass ornaments, garlands and beautiful tinsel. She then laid a manger at his feet with a small baby that had been wrapped in swaddling clothes. A loving mother and father were set up as if they were admiring the baby. Magi and an assortment of sheep, cows and donkeys were placed in the snow just outside the proud parents.

The bench was now the center attraction of the entire village as people, both young and old, passed by to admire the newborn babe. Nobody threw rocks this time and even a choir stood by singing praise to the baby who was some kind of special king. The bench watched all the smiling faces that peaked out from under the colorful scarves wrapped tightly against their necks. But it wasn't until the preacher arrived and began reading from a special book that the bench understood who the baby was. He was the Son of God and prophesied Messiah that was given as a gift to the entire world!

Forgetfulness

As I sat there, glancing out at the rain in the stillness of the early morning, I suddenly remembered that I had unfailingly forgotten to set my clock forward an hour. So when I looked at the clock, which digitally and joyfully lit up red proclaiming it was eight o' clock it was in fact nine. I detest having to reset all the clocks in my house twice a year and think that whoever came up with the idea of daylight savings time should be keelhauled, that is if a ship of considerable enough breadth can be located.

Usually, the realization that I had forgotten this small, seemly insignificant fact and now would be late for church wasn't such an immense problem. The whole slipup just meant I could just lie around in bed for a few more hours and enjoy a book, catch up on the news or finish a crossword, however, as the main speaker who was supposed to be standing behind the pulpit in an hour I was immediately gripped with fear.

Forgetting to do something like take out the trash, make my bed or squirt liquid lubricant on the bathroom door hinges doesn't usually make me panic and run for the trashcan but when a hundred or so people sitting in a church somewhere staring blankly at the front wall, well, you get the idea.

I still had time to get there, if I could just change into my clothes as fast as Superman. Quickly, while shoving my leg into my trousers, I began to go over the calculations in my head; five minutes to dress, three minutes to brush my hair and teeth allowing twenty-five minutes to drive to church just as the musicians and singers were finishing up with worship.

Around the same time my blood pressure was beginning to subside I realized my lovely wife had straightened up the house and was now punishing me for being a slob by hiding my sermon notes somewhere in the house.

Reworking my calculations I discovered that I had not anticipated this latest turn of events allotting extra time to complete a search and rescue mission for my missing papers. As I frantically hunted for my notes I managed to step on the cat's tail, bump into the dog and run into the corner of a poorly positioned living room coffee table.

As I stood there throbbing with pain, half dressed, I thought that if the daylight savings time guy or girl was still alive and could be found I might have to haul them over the keel twice.

Forgetfulness is no laughing matter, especially when it comes to leaving a pan on the stove with hot oil. Next on the list would be forgetting to pick someone up from somewhere which comes in at a close third but the absolute worst thing to forget about is spending time with God.

Life today is so busy that at lunch time we often either hastily pull in for fast food or skip it altogether. We have so many diversions to distract us that many times neglect to pray, read our bibles or attend a weekly study. Spending time with our Creator has unfortunately fallen to the bottom of our lists and if you're anything like me then you don't even have a bottom to your list.

King Solomon once stated "Remember your Creator before the silver cord is loosed, or the golden bowl is broken, or the pitcher shattered at the fountain, or the wheel broken at the well. Then the dust will return to the earth as it was, and the spirit will return to God who gave it."

Our days here on earth are numbered and there are only so many breaths we will take in. Therefore, we should make the most of our time for the years are destructive and corrosive. Too many of us continue to throw caution to the winds of time blatantly ignoring the warnings God continually puts in front of us.

He has set us in this world for only a short time. We are merely pilgrims passing through on our way to eternity. Our lives are like vapor which is seen one moment then gone the next. Where we will spend eternity depends on what we do with our time we spend with our Creator. Putting God first in our lives, making time with Him a priority is a great place to start.

"For God so loved the world that He gave His only begotten Son that whoever should believe in Him would not perish but have everlasting life."

So while forgetting to set the clock forward might make you late for an appointment, forgetting about God and His Son Jesus Christ will make you miss eternity.

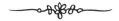

Turning around

It has been said that when a nation begins to decline, that morality, respect for others and virtuous living become absent or nonexistent within their population. The nation of Israel went through this same cycle over and over again. When their situation in life worsened they would call upon their high priest to make intersession for them through sacrifice and prayer. Unfortunately, before they came to this point they would often turn their backs, falling away from the God of all creation.

Some theologians suggest that the nation of Israel can be looked at as the unfaithful wife of Jehovah. The nation, once they began to worship other gods, putting their trust in idols made of earth, wood or stone, set themselves on a path towards destruction and judgment. Many believe America to be on the same road to destruction as we watch substance abuse, abortion as well as violent crime escalate. Basic human rights, common decency and love for one another appear to be on the decline.

At America's roots was as a dream, a grand idea, a city set on a hill, which would give light to the entire world. My family was part of that expedition and is represented by two separate signers on the "Mayflower Compact." The "Mayflower Compact" was signed on 11 November 1620 onboard the Mayflower shortly after the ship came to anchor off Provincetown Harbor.

Israel also shared America's dream of being governed by God, a city set on a hill and a light to the entire world. Unfortunately, the nation had fallen into the same moral decline and complacency that is evident in our country today.

In Jewish history we see that between the period after the Judges and before the Kings that the children of Jacob had turned from following the God of their father's and began worshipping idols; gods of earth, wood and stone. The nation's decline also produced immorality beyond our comprehension which included false religious practices, temple prostitution and child sacrifice. They had turned away from fellowship with God, to godless practices neglecting His presence as well as His guidance for their nation.

Within the pages of 1 Samuel 5:1-6:21 there is a story where the Israelites go into battle with the Philistines without first asking for God's guidance. The result is their defeat as four thousand of Israel's finest soldiers perish on the battlefield. The fledgling nation's elders discuss why the Lord allowed them to be defeated? One of the elders suggest to haul the Ark of the Covenant from Shiloh into battle with them; believing that because God's presence was somehow contained inside the gilded box, that through this superstitious power they would be able to now conquer their enemies.

This decision, not only results in their defeat with many more soldiers dying, but allows their enemy to capture the Ark of the Covenant. The Ark, which was the place where God's Shekinah Glory would hover over the mercy seat, was now in their enemy's hands. As with any spoils of war the victors hauled their trophy back to their capitol city, Ashdod, setting it in their temple next to their deity. Early the next morning, they discover their god lying face down on the ground before the Ark. Puzzled, they set it up again only to find, the following morning, their idol lying face down on the ground with its head and both hands broken off.

Our God has a wonderful sense of humor! Can you just imagine this picture of the Philistine's half fish, half man god lying face down in a posture of worship directly in front of the Ark of the Covenant of the Lord?

The "take away" is that we should only put our trust in the Lord! Praying and seeking His guidance is paramount to a healthy, successful and prosperous life. Proverbs 3:5, 6 NKJV says "Trust in the Lord with all your heart, and lean not on your own understanding; in all your ways acknowledge Him, and He shall direct your paths."

I have made this section of Old Testament scripture my personal "life verse". If we stay close to God and allow Him to guide our lives then we will not fall into a pitfall of superstition and arrogance. It is only when we continue to trust in God, His authority as well as in His Son, Jesus, that we will prosper living in our new resurrected life.

God, the Creator of heaven and earth, cannot be contained in a box. The world's only true hope, our nation's only true hope is a right relationship with our God. When we begin to make God our priority by seeking His will, His kingdom then and only then will He hear our prayers and heal our land.

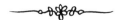

Pots and pans

It turned midnight as the last pot was washed, rinsed and placed back up on the galley rack that hung above the grill in the kitchen. The head chef, sous chef and prep assistant also hung up their aprons on the hooks by the door then switched of the lights and locked the door to the kitchen.

There had been a good turn out that night, the poached salmon, sautéed leeks and garlic sorbet had been a great hit and sold out within the first few hours of the evening meal. Although the head chef hadn't anticipated this, he had a backup plan to serve pasta ala nirvana.

Now that all three of the chefs had retired, the kitchen cleansed and locked for the night something magical began to happen. One by one each pot, pan, cup and saucer began to come to life.

It wasn't long before the entire kitchen was buzzing with life as several coffee cups began talking to the wine glasses and several large soup pots discussed the chef's careful preparation of their contents. While the frying pans raved about the poached the salmon the pots discussed the pasta.

"It was our final, great contribution that made the dinner a success!" said the wine glasses that had held the garlic sorbet.

"No, it was the sautéed leeks that captured our customer's culinary imagination." replied the sauce pans proudly as the bowls that held the raspberry glaze listened intently.

The pots that had held the pasta boldly replied that it was their pasta nirvana that had rescued the evening from utter failure. The tension in the kitchen was so thick that you could have cut it with a knife and it seemed for moment that an all-out culinary war was on the verge of breaking out that night.

Soon razor sharp knives were standing at attention on the stainless counter in perfect formation, row after row. The meat tenderizers too were at the ready as well as several meat cleavers that were positioned to fall onto several wine glasses below.

Hatred, jealousy and envy were boiling up everywhere like thick, rich brown gravy that had been left on too high of heat and was getting dangerously close to spilling over the edge of a sauce pan.

One by one, the spices jumped out of the rack; cayenne pepper, salt, cumin and several tins of chili powder. The lines were being drawn and attack plans were being discussed as the first light of dawn began streaming through the windows above the food pantry.

As morning dawned, everyone had gone their own way while strife and division were the only items on today's menu. Each kitchen utensil, pot, cup and pan thought that their way was the only true way of salvation.

In this kitchen analogy, division arises when one group thinks that they have special revelation or that their recipe to reach heaven is mixed using only their ingredients and utensils.

Today there exist many groups of well-intentioned people who, while calling and rallying for unity, exclude others who they feel don't measure up. They are blind to the fact that love is the universal ingredient that needs to be poured out, sprinkled and dashed out everywhere to everyone.

The early church began with several Jewish fishermen, tradesmen, zealots and a tax collector. The church was born as Jesus Christ promised to send God's Spirit to the entire world to come along side and convict people of wrong living and their need for God's love.

Unfortunately, God's simple message to believe on the name of His Son Jesus Christ and to love one another has been changed and what was the simple gospel of good news has been changed into many different gospels; inventions of men.

Logic demands that there can only be One, True and Living God. It also insists that there can only be one path to reach that God and not several roads arriving safely at heaven's eternal home.

The gods that some create, the idols that some worship have no substance or reality to the holy and almighty God who created the universe in which we live. There is only one true church and Jesus Christ is the Head of that body and the eternal King of heaven and earth.

Unfortunately, the world's religions as well as Christian denominations continue to split, divide and argue over the particular ingredients of their faiths. However, the fact remains that there still exists only one true chef who runs the kitchen.

In the end it really doesn't matter what the pots and pans have to say but what the head chef has commanded "I am the way, the truth, and the life. No one comes to the Father except through Me."

Clutter

Pastor David's office has always looked like a hurricane had ransacked it or a bomb went off in it. The strong winds or person responsible left everything in unorganized piles around some sort of pedestal that could have been a desk. For some unknown and peculiar reason Pastor David once gave me a key to his office. Thinking back on his decision I can't be sure if he was in his right mind when he handed over the key which I still have in my possession.

It was like handing a kid the key to a candy store and walking away in complete trust that the kid wouldn't steal any of the candy piled up inside. I remember as a younger man unlocking the door, squeezing down the narrowing hallway which had piles of books and unopened mail stacked on either side. I was in heaven with a plethora of bible commentaries, textbooks and books written in both Greek and Hebrew which were fun to hold upside down while pretending to read them.

Only a handful of people had a key and even out of those only a few were brave enough to venture into his office without a guide. Even the pastor's secretary would stand just inside the doorway and converse with him careful not to take too many steps into the jungle of book- vines that had grown up both walls of the office landscape.

It was different for me because I loved being able to lock myself in his office in a secret hall of knowledge where I could read all about Jesus, His disciples and works by the early Church Fathers. On one occasion, I discovered part of a couch peeking through a large pile of mail and several cases of diet coke cans. I was able to push some of the debris off unto the cluttered floor and lay down in sort of prone position with my feet on top of the cases of diet coke. I always locked the door behind me so that no one would disturb me, as was the habit of the local parishioners.

Of course, I'm looking back thirty years and haven't actually been into David's office for a long while. I remember it was a special place for me where the Spirit of God would guide me as I turned the pages of Matthew Henry, J. Vernon McGee or G. Campbell Morgan. As a young man I wanted desperately to understand the deep mysteries of God that were concealed in all the books that were piled around me.

Today I find myself lost in another jungle of books. These books I know intimately because I have purchased all of them while only managing to read a few cover to cover. Many of my books I've wanted to finish but just couldn't get into the story while others remained too lofty in their presentation to keep my attention for more than a few minutes. While staring at the many piles of books in my office something dawned on me.

I don't think Jesus would have read any copy on systematic theology. In my arrogance to learn, more I had acquired volumes of books on how to study the New Testament, commentaries on the Old Testament and volumes of study helps which were in stacks lining the walls of my office. It's strange but I have a guilty feeling while reading books that just don't make any sense to me.

The truth is book studies, guides and extra biblical resources take us away from the leading of the Holy Spirit through the books that make up the Old and New Testaments. Religious leaders of Jesus' day were so caught up in their pursuit of knowledge that they missed the first appearance of the Messiah.

Pride is our downfall. I have seen it rear its ugly head in myself and I have seen it in many other Christians I know. Jesus taught that what we need to do is demonstrate love and not just simply talk about it. Even our high school English teachers would say that "love" is a verb and depicts action. Jesus demonstrated His love for us when He offered Himself up as a sacrifice; the Lamb of God.

It's difficult to understand how volumes of works have been written on what Jesus taught. Jesus Himself simply encouraged us to love God with all our hearts, minds and strength then to love our neighbors as ourselves.

While I have made the decision to throw out most of my books on theology, which are piled up on the floor, I will still hold onto a few of my favorites. Beloved let us not only love in word but also in deed with every opportunity that God presents to us.

Loving others

The store is crowded today. I'm running behind in my schedule so I rush through the sliding doors to get ahead of several other people who were walking in front of me. While looking down at my shopping list I turn a corner sharply and bump into an elderly lady who was surveying the shelves for pickled okra. As we collide, her glasses fall to the ground.

Embarrassed, I quickly say "I'm sorry" and pick up her frames off the floor. She has a frown on her face and doesn't seem to notice that one of her lenses is missing but I don't have time to wait for a scolding so I hurry on my way.

Shortly, I'm ready to leave but all lines are backed up. I rush to the only open self-serve kiosk pushing myself in front of a clean cut, young man wearing mechanics overalls. He looks a bit miffed and irritated but I'm too late to be sympathetic or courteous so I punch the English button and scan my items. As I key in my pin number, several customers begin inching their way forward practically breathing down my neck like a pack of wolves.

But I'm losing time and need to get to work, so I shoot out the door leaving my cart in front of them at the kiosk. As I rush out, I whisk past several girl scouts selling cookies at a table. On the fly they smile and ask me if I could support their troop, but I'm in a hurry so I pat my pockets and say I'm out of cash, feeling my money clip that is full of cash. One of their dad's is dressed in his patrolman's uniform and gives me a sullen look as I dart past. I turn around just in time to see an SUV slamming on the brakes. Then looking down at my wristwatch and back at the driver I shake my fist at them and trip over the island curb.

Shaken, I survey the parking lot and notice the elderly lady with the missing lens pushing her shopping cart into the cart corral. She misses the opening by half a cart, opens the door of her 63' Bel Air coup and sinks down to the exact height of the dashboard. Meanwhile her cart begins to slowly roll away. As the cart picks up momentum, I realize it is pointed directly at my car. I know in my mind that if I could fly I still would never make it in time.

While looking at the new dent in my door, I watch the Chevy Bel Air getting away. I begin pursuit and speed through a school zone going slightly over 45 miles an hour. Several parents honk their horns at me to slow down but I'm losing sight of the perpetrator and push the accelerator to the floor. Something catches my eye in my rear view mirror and I watch in horror as the flashing red lights of the patrol car invite me to pull over.

"Where's the fire?" asks the patrolman with a smile as he begins writing in his little yellow ticket book. I tell him about the okra lady, the runaway shopping cart and the new dent in my door. He removes his sunglasses and glares at me "Do you know how fast you were going? No?, well I do, because I've been following you since you pulled out from the grocery store."

Thirty minutes later, after the patrolman finished an impromptu vehicle safety inspection, I pull back out into traffic, down the street, around a corner and into my office parking space. I briskly ran up several flights of stairs to the main hallway. After several steps, I arrive at my office where a clean cut, young man dressed in mechanics overalls is standing in the doorway.

"Sorry mister, the men's bathroom overflowed into your office. We are evacuating the sludge now and then will be taking out the carpet, so you won't be able to enter for at least a couple of hours," said the familiar face of the young man that I think I had seen earlier that day.

I didn't even bother to ask if he would do me a favor and let me in. Sitting down in the hallway, I opened my briefcase, took out my work for that day and began working on the chapter I would be teaching on Sunday. "Love suffers long *and* is kind; love does not envy; love does not parade itself, is not puffed up; does not behave rudely, does not seek its own, is not provoked, thinks no evil; does not rejoice in iniquity, but rejoices in the truth; bears all things, believes all things, hopes all things, endures all things." 1 Corinthians 13 NKJV.

Eight hundred words through the bible

In the beginning God created everything we see around us from nothing. He made a man in His image and then from the rib of the man created a woman to complete Him. In order to know if the man and the woman would love Him, God allowed them to be tempted by a fallen archangel. The man and the woman sin as God sets a curse on humanity but also promising to send the solution in the form of the Blessed Redeemer or Messiah. God covers the couples' nakedness with the skins of animals the man was entrusted to care for and instructs them on the correct way to worship and how to approach Him.

In the process of time, two brothers are born. One obeys God in the acceptable way to worship by bringing a lamb to the altar while the other brother attempts to worship God in his own way by bringing the fruit of the field. When his sacrifice is rejected, jealousy fills his countenance as he murders his brother. Meanwhile the earth is becoming filled with selfish, destructive people who have completely turned their back on their Creator. God shows His grace and mercy and saves a small remnant that love and trust in Him, as the heavenly floodgates and fountains of the deep open up, covering the earth in a catastrophic worldwide deluge.

Safe aboard the ark, eight people wait for God's deliverance as a dove returns with an olive branch in its mouth. Once again God blesses His creation and commands them to go spread out and fill the entire earth, promising never again to destroy the earth with water. Generations pass as people forget about God and decide that the fertile plain below the ark is probably a better place to stay, build cities and towers to their newly invented gods of creation; gods made of earth, wood and stone.

God, wanting to reveal Himself to the entire world, chooses one family line through which the promised Savior would come into the world. God promises that his family would prosper, eventually becoming as numerous as the stars in heaven or the sands of the seashore. One descendant is blessed with twelve sons who become the twelve tribes of this new God-led nation.

The youngest son, being mistreated by his other brothers, is sold into slavery and bought by a wealthy

Egyptian noble. Because of his obedience to the One True and Living God he is blessed and prospers, eventually becoming second in command of the entire Egyptian nation. In God's time, a famine devours the entire land of Canaan, forcing the other brothers to look for food down in Egypt. Unknowingly, they are granted an audience with their brother who they do not recognize. They end up being fed, cared for and eventually relocate to Goshen, Egypt.

Four hundred and thirty-two years pass as the small family of twelve brothers grows into a nation of Hebrew slaves. Because of their growing out-of-control population, the Pharaoh commands that all male children be thrown into the Nile River. One male baby escapes death by being put into a small ark of bulrushes and floated down the river where the Pharaoh's daughter finds him. This Hebrew baby grows up as one of Pharaoh's own sons with all the luxury and entitlement that one can dream of.

When he is older, he kills an Egyptian who is beating a Hebrew slave. Now the young man is banished from Egypt and escapes into the desert of Midian. At the age of eighty, the shepherd is sent back to Egypt to demand that the Pharaoh let his people go! After ten plagues that were focused on the Egyptian gods of nature, gods of wood and stone, the death of the first born is the last straw as Pharaoh lets the fledgling nation of Israel go.

The people grumble and complain and are sentenced to walk for forty years in the desert. After this generation passes, they are allowed to go into the Promised Land. Soon mighty kings are building a very large and powerful nation. However, they once again forget the God who has led them there and begin to worship the gods of nature; gods of wood and stone.

So, when the moment was right, God sent His own Son. He opened the way so that everyone who had hoped and believed that when time was done, God would be able to make us one! But the selfish and destructive people grabbed hold of the Son of God and they beat Him, mocking Him until He died as the angry crowd nailed Him to a tree.

So the curse that started in a garden ended as a gift on a cross.

The family line

Our family grew this year with the addition of a new daughter and our first born grandson. The Lord is good and this Thanksgiving was a reminder of just how good He really is. Our table was packed full of a variety of foods whose presentation mesmerized our senses. We welcomed a slight winter's chill by all who have just endured a ninety-six degree Thanksgiving Day.

Now that Thanksgiving is over its time to wake up all our Christmas decorations from their long summer's nap. Boxes of all sizes will begin tumbling down from the mezzanine as brightly colored ornaments make their annual appearance adorning walls, Christmas trees and the gables of our homes.

Grandpa, who is turning ninety this next year, set up the timer to the twenty foot tall, six pointed lighted star that rests year round on the peak of his roof. Next Sunday we will make the long drive to the coast to hear a group of community singers perform Handel's Messiah.

Even coffee shops and fast food establishments are getting into the Christmas spirit pulling out their seasonal secret recipes as soup kitchens begin to plan for the large crowds that will line up around the block for another free meal. Bright red, kettles will begin popping up all over town so be sure to put a couple extra dollars in them to help feed our cities homeless and less fortunate.

The thing I love most about Christmas is that for this next month we not only prepare our homes and businesses for Christmas but we also prepare our hearts to receive God's own gift to the world. You might not know this, but the gift of God was the giving of His own Son to redeem the world from sin.

I have discovered something special during my forty-two years of studying the bible. Its true it is a love letter from God to the world but it's also living, active and sharper than a double edged sword. It is a record of one specific family line that started with Adam and Eve and follows this one family all the way to the virgin birth of God's own Son. The bible is filled with prophecy, written long before the birth of Jesus of Nazareth.

The Old Testament is a genealogical record, specifically describing one family line. We follow that family line onto the ark as the world is destroyed by water. Then through Noah's son Shem we read as Father Abraham is born from the family of Eber which later is known as the Hebrews.

The genealogy continues through Abraham sons Isaac and Jacob. From Jacob's twelve sons the twelve tribes of Israel are born giving birth to a new nation which was ruled by God. The line of kings for of this new nation would come from one of Jacob's sons who was named Judah.

Now the family line that the Messiah would come from narrows further. From the root of Jesse, he would come through his son David. God even narrows the requirements further as he curses Solomon's kingly line saying "none of your sons will prosper sitting on the throne of David."

Now in the books of Matthew and Luke you will find two genealogies that most ministers skip over and don't study. These genealogies are important. The one in Matthew is Joseph's the step-father of Jesus and the one in Luke is the one we want to study because it is Mary's the mother of Jesus.

Mary and Joseph are both related to King David but Joseph is related through David's son Solomon while Mary is related to David though David's son Nathan. What's the big deal? Jesus would have been disqualified as the Messiah if he had been blood related through David's son Solomon.

God's promise to redeem us through the virgin birth of His Son was the main reason we have the inspired canonized books that make up the bible. "Faith comes by hearing and hearing by the word of God." The more you read and study the bible you will begin to see this connection. It's undoubtedly undeniable.

"Now faith is the substance of things hoped for, the evidence of things not seen." We don't follow after some figment of our imagination or fairly tale hero while desperately wishing he was real. No, our faith has substance and evidence for the birth of Jesus, His death as well as His resurrection.

But faith comes by hearing and hearing by the word of God, so unless you're willing to commit to study and dig in to the word of God your faith will remain weak.

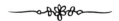

Passover

As December quickly approaches soon boxes of colored Christmas lights and ornaments will be hauled out from their dusty resting places in our attics. Beautiful colored glass bulbs and lights will not only begin to fill and illuminate our homes but will also remind us of another very beautiful and bright light that 2000 years ago appeared in the world to bring us all hope and salvation. Christmas is, without a doubt, my most very favorite holiday and season of the year. It is a great opportunity for the entire world to celebrate the birth of the Messiah, our Emmanuel (God with us). God Himself actually being born into His own creation to provide the only "Way" for all men to one day be in His most awesome presence.

It's interesting to note, that even in Nepal other religions celebrate Christmas. While in Nepal I was told that some Hindus and Buddhists celebrate Christmas by setting up a tree with colorful decorations and exchange gifts with one another. These people in a very traditional way even without being part of the larger universal church of Jesus Christ celebrate His birth. They honor Jesus even while following their own gods and religious practices, taking the time to acknowledge Jesus Christ, who they admit was God's great gift to the world. The good news of Jesus

Christ being born is the greatest story that will ever be told anywhere in this universe. It is paramount to understanding how "we" as fallen, sinful human beings can be restored back to fellowship with a holy and righteous God.

As we continue our study in the book of Exodus and before moving on through the Red Sea crossing I believe it to be very important to take another look at the institution of Passover. We left off just before Pharaoh let the Israelites leave which is found in Exodus 12:21-28. What is most curious to me is how God imbedded the role and mission of the Messiah and His plan for salvation into this extremely important festival in the Old Testament and Judaism. It can't be overstated and would be sad if overlooked how God's plan of redemption was concealed in the Old Testament scriptures.

In Exodus 12:21 Moses is now instructing all the elders of Israel to prepare for their family's salvation and deliverance from their 430 years of bondage in Egypt. They were to take a lamb from the flock on the tenth day of Nissan and keep it in their homes until the fourteenth day. Here's a question for you all, what happens to animals we bring into our homes? Children immediately begin playing and naming the animal and soon it becomes a pet, a pet that unfortunately will be brutally slaughtered in just four short days. The idea God is trying to get through to the Israelites and to us is that our salvation comes at a very high cost. It wouldn't be until Jesus would arrive on earth that the stark reality of the Passover convocation would come into complete focus. Even as the nails are being driven into Jesus' hands and feet and as they watched Him die they wondered if they had miss placed their faith in Him.

God instructed the head of each family to kill the Passover lamb. Then they were to take a bunch of Hyssop, dip it in the blood and strike both the lentil and doorposts of their home. In the gospel of John 19:29 we have additional information concerning the use of a Hyssop plant that was used to offer Jesus wine vinegar. Here the Israelites were to strike the wooden members, which supported the doorway or entrance to the house, with the blood from the lamb. In the very same way God invites us to apply the blood of Jesus to the lentil and doorposts of our own hearts securing our place in His presence. What a picture the Passover gives us of how one day the actual Lamb of God, Jesus Christ, would shed His own blood on that old wooden, rugged cross that stood on Calvary.

The passage goes on to say how the Lord would not allow the destroyer to come into the Israelite's houses and strike them down. Once we put our faith, trust into Jesus we are sealed by the Holy Spirit and the destroyer has no more power or claim to our souls. The bible teaches that no one or can pluck us out of His hands. And so the Passover was to be an everlasting ordinance forever to be observed and remembered for eternity. So as we pull out the dusty boxes filled with garland and bows, colored lights, nativity scenes and all our favorite trapping of the Christmas season let us remember the Passover Lamb, Jesus Christ who became the brightest light of all.

Walls of separation

"For the message of the cross is foolishness to those who are perishing, but to us who are being saved it is the power of God" said Paul to the people who had gathered at the synagogue to hear what he had to say.

Then one man in back of the room said "but I follow Apollos for he is a gifted, scholarly man from Alexandria" and another man stood up and said "I follow Barnabas for he was chosen by God" and yet another stood up and said "I follow Paul for he was visited by the Messiah in a vision on the road to Damascus".

However, there were also those assembled there that day, in the synagogue, who did not believe in Jesus to be the Messiah and when they heard the things spoken of by Paul they were filled with envy; and contradicting and blaspheming, they opposed the things spoken by Paul.

"It was necessary that the word of God should be spoken to you first; but since you reject it, and judge yourself unworthy of everlasting life, behold, we turn to the gentiles. For the Lord has commanded us." said Paul who spoke with boldness to everyone gathered around him in the synagogue.

Solomon was right, there really isn't anything new under the sun. People have been arguing about religion, the existence of an all-powerful God for millennia. Wars and crusades have raged all over the world at the expense of innocent lives. Various conflicts over Catholicism verses Protestantism have maimed and killed the young and the old and continue to this day in some areas of the world. Even the Lord, Jesus Christ, was put on trial, condemned to death because He dared to tell the religious leaders of His day the truth about God's love for mankind.

These religious leaders insisted on following rigid and strict rules to the point where they ignored people's needs while assembling religious systems for their own profit. They would go through a variety of religious practices even praying loudly hoping that people would notice. Jesus once asked these men why they spent so much time cleaning the outside of their cup while the inside remained filthy. Simply put religion is man's attempt to reach an all powerful, all knowing eternal God. Man in his arrogance and pride embraced religion over the relationship that God had always intended to have with his creation.

Instead, men have constructed denominational walls of separation while turning their backs on God's simple message of love. Things haven't really changed much today? Look around and you will find many religious systems that have been built on other men's dogma and contrived theology. Even within some mainstream evangelical organizations we find the same legalism and lust for gathering large amounts assets; a practice that was increasing in Jesus' time. No, religion will fail us every time and it will only be through God's message of love, having a relationship with His Son Jesus Christ, that will be the world's only true hope.

In Jesus' time, He handpicked twelve uneducated men made up of fishermen, shepherds and tax collectors to witness how God was going to save the world. Even at that time, they jockeyed for position in their own little group, while Jesus was preparing to demonstrate what God's love is really all about. They were proud; one of the Masters' chosen twelve but none of them understood what Jesus was trying to teach them. Jesus even gave them opportunity to prove themselves during the last Passover Feast when they all pasted by the towel and water jug that was strategically positioned by the front door. You see, they were all too important to stoop to the lowest position of a household slave. One by one they passed by without washing one another's feet.

"He humbled Himself and became obedient to the point of death, even the death of the cross. For the message of the cross is foolishness to those who are perishing, but to us who are being saved it is the power of God"

So pride is our downfall, our mortal enemy and we will all struggle fighting against its power over our lives. I have witnessed myself, leaders in the church, men who God allowed to handle huge amounts of responsibility only to fall and cave under the weight of building their own kingdoms and reputations. That's why I don't look to men for the answers but keep my eyes steadily fastened on our Lord Jesus Christ, who is both the author and finisher of our salvation.

"But the natural man does not receive the things of the Spirit of God, for they are foolishness to him; nor can he know them, because they are spiritually discerned." 1 Corinthians 2:15 NKJV.

In the blink of an eye

It's a rainy January morning on a bridge in Texas. A Baptist minister is heading home from a Christian conference. His window is rolled down as the cool rain blowing in both refreshes and keeps him alert as he drives the last few miles home. His thoughts keep replaying visuals of his wife and children and the great love that he has for them. In the blink of an eye a large semi tractor-trailer swerves and rolls over the minister's compact car, crushing it like a trash compactor.

Emergency personal are called and respond but no pulse can be found anywhere on the victim's limp body. A yellow tarp is spread out over mangled body temporarily hiding it from onlookers who have gotten out of their vehicles to assess the situation. The bridge is the only way over the river as traffic comes to a halt and begins to back up in both directions. In another car, a short distance away, another pastor gets out of his car and walks over to the accident where he asks to pray for the victim.

"He's dead, I'm afraid your prayers won't be of any use to him." says the fireman as he motions the man to get back across the yellow ribbon.

"If you don't mind I'm a pastor and I like to say prayers for the victim and his family anyway" replied the pastor firmly.

"Sure, go ahead but the body has been crushed and it's not a pretty sight in there." cautioned the fireman.

The pastor reaches through the window of the smashed car, grabs the hand of the deceased and begins to pray. An hour and a half later, after the initial accident, life miraculously returns to the dead body. It was a miracle; however, it will take years of excruciating orthopedic therapy before regaining the use of his arms and legs.

So where did the minister's spirit go while the car was smashed on the bridge for an hour and a half?

The minister says he didn't flow through a long dark tunnel. He didn't have a sensation of fading away or coming back. He does say that a light enveloped him with brilliance beyond what we know here on earth. He felt joy, love and warmth like he had never felt before. A large crowd of family and friends were there to meet him. They exchanged hugs, kisses and handshakes, it was a real family reunion in a truly perfect place!

Then he heard the praise and worship. The heavenly music was composed of a myriad of songs, choruses and hymns which filled the air with praise to God and the Lamb for His grace and mercy. There were no sad songs of suffering and death only songs of joy to God the King.

The minister goes on to describe how the crowd was walking with him towards a huge wall that seemed like it went on forever in three directions. As they walked up to the wall they stopped just outside a gate that was iridescent or pearlescent in appearance. Looking through the gate towards the inside, the light was even more brilliant, if that was even possible, and he could see a golden city where even the streets where paved with golden bricks.

In the revelation Jesus Christ gave to the apostle John, he writes "The construction of its wall was of jasper; and the city was pure gold, like clear glass. The foundations of the wall of the city were adorned with all kinds of precious stones" Then John describes the gates "The twelve gates were twelve pearls: each individual gate was of one pearl. And the street of the city was pure gold, like transparent glass."

I don't know about you but I'm looking forward to walking through those pearlescent gates and into the light of God! Only then, will we dwell with God and be His people. God will wipe away every tear from our eyes and there will be no more death, nor sorrow, nor crying or pain. For the former things will have passed away! Halleluiah!

So you may ask "What's all this going to cost me?"

Actually, it will cost you nothing. God's plan, all along, even from before our beginning was to redeem His creation through Himself. Sound strange? Not really, even the name "Jesus" in its Hebrew form "Jeshua or Joshua" literally means "Yahweh is salvation" or "Yahweh delivered".

So here is the gazillion dollar question...Are you ready to enter in through those pearlescent gates? Believing in Jesus Christ means that you are putting your faith in and trust Him to be the means by which you enter in. I hope you consider God's invitation and receive His free gift of salvation this very moment.

Broken hearted

The hurt was still too fresh. The pain was too deep. Trevor and Elise tried desperately to cope with the events of the last few months; the death of their children. They couldn't sleep, couldn't eat and there were several trays of food from friends and neighbors spoiling in the refrigerator. Every time Elise fell asleep she had dreams of the catastrophe and would automatically wake herself up. Trevor had trouble focusing at work and when he was home, well; he wasn't much help or strength to his wife in fact it was hard just to look at each other.

Grieving hurt like nothing they had ever experienced and the world seemed to keep moving on without them. They were tired of explaining details to well wishers it just made everything worse. It was hard to believe how much it hurt and found it much easier to be isolated, locked up in their home. The pastor had made several visits, church elders and family had flown in from all over the United States to stay with them but nothing made the hurt go away.

Going to get the mail became an unwanted task, a daily reminder as cards and letters kept pouring in from all over the country as their situation had made the national news. Their only children were gone, they had nothing left to live for, they even talked about ending it all. One day Trevor picked up a bible he had thrown against a wall during a fit of rage. He looked down at it. It lay on the floor folded open and creased on a passage in second Corinthians chapter five.

"For we know that if our earthly house, this tent, is destroyed, we have a building from God, a house not made with hands, eternal in the heavens. For in this we groan, earnestly desiring to be clothed with our habitation which is from heaven, if indeed, having been clothed, we shall not be found naked. For we who are in this tent groan, being burdened, not because we want to be unclothed, but further clothed, that mortality may be swallowed up by life.

Now He who has prepared us for this very thing is God, who also has given us the Spirit as a guarantee.

So we are always confident, knowing that while we are at home in the body we are absent from the Lord. For we walk by faith, not by sight. We are confident, yes, well pleased rather to be absent from the body and to be present with the Lord." 2 Corinthians 5:1-8 NJKV.

"To be absent from the body is to be present with the lord" Trevor kept saying those words over and over again as a wonderful feeling came pouring over him. God spoke to Trevor's heart that night through the power of His Holy Spirit. Trevor had heard God's soft voice, speaking to his heart; his children were with Him, safe and completely healed. At that very moment, he felt a weight physically lift from his shoulders and immediately he breathed freely once again.

He ran to find his wife and shared the passage. Elise thought for a moment and then the two prayed together.

"Oh gracious God, God of the heavens and the earth we thank you for revealing Your plan to us through Your word. Only You are faithful and true, You are the first and the last, the beginning and the end. Through the giving of Your own Son we are forgiven, totally forgiven. We both thank you for healing our children and for knowing nothing can separate them from Your love! In Jesus name we pray." They fell down onto their bed, wept and felt as if God had touched them both in a very personal way through His Spirit.

Jesus warned us that in this world there would be trials and tribulation. He went on to say that we should be of good cheer because He has overcome this world. When Jesus was being interrogated by Pilate, He told him that

His kingdom was not of this world. In fact, the apostle Paul said that no eye has seen, no ear has heard what wonderful things the Lord has planned for us to share in eternity. All we must do to receive this free gift from God is to ask Him. The fact is if you have to work for your salvation then it's not much of a gift, is it?

So if your grieving for a lost loved one, believe with all your heart that God has a plan and nothing can stop it. The Messiah's return is imminent, right at the gates and soon we shall see His face, our loved ones and His promised kingdom which is not of this world.

Just a comma

The young rabbi was barely thirty-two years old but the appearance of his hands made him look fifty. They were rough, leather worn and scarred from many years of sawing, chiseling and general carpentry work with his father Joseph. He had just returned to Nazareth from a trip he had taken around the Sea of Galilee with a couple close friends. The young rabbi had been gaining popularity over the last couple of months while rumors of him performing miracles began to circulate. It was said all the young man had to do was just touch someone and they were healed! These stories had taken birth when an old leper had showed up at the temple to present his body for inspection and to offer the required sacrifice for his cleansing.

The trip around the great inland sea had taken several weeks and every day the villages would be filled with crowds wanting to see, listen to and some had hopes of being touched by this newly discovered prophet. There hadn't been this much of a ruckus since John started baptizing down by the Jordan River a couple of years ago. Many eyewitnesses to these miracles believed this man had an anointing from God but the skeptics outnumbered them and there was even a small gathering that had begun plotting against his apparent popularity.

The hot summer winds had withered all but the sturdiest late spring wild flowers. Yellow flax and white trumpet flowers dotted the hillside as Jesus left Galilee to return home to Nazareth. He was alone now as his two traveling companions from home had stayed at a relative's home in Capernaum. The winds on this uphill stretch of road whipped violently at an endless landscape of tall swaying grass. It swirled and twirled the long grass into cyclonic eddies that reminded Jesus of turbulent ocean waves he remembered seeing along the western coast.

Jesus grabbed the leather strap holding the skin, filled with water, on his back and poured some down his parched throat. The blowing dust had also made his eyes hurt as he washed them with some of the water before returning the skin to his shoulder. Some fishermen had offered him some dried fish that they were drying in the sun, as he had left the last village at the water's edge. It tasted wonderful and as he chewed on the dry, salted meat he remembered the men's kindness. Surely, he would be back this way and offer them something in return.

With any luck he would be home in Nazareth before nightfall. His mother Mary still lived in the family's ancestral home that had an attached workshop his father had built. Sadly, Joseph had passed on a few years ago from some unknown reason. Now it was Jesus' and James's responsibility to take care of their mother. As he walked he remembered that tomorrow was the Sabbath and how he had been looking forward to attending the morning reading in the village's synagogue with his mother and brother.

"Then Jesus returned in the power of the Spirit to Galilee, and news of Him went out through all the surrounding region. And He taught in their synagogues, being glorified by all. So He came to Nazareth, where He had been brought up. And as His custom was, He went into the synagogue on the Sabbath day, and stood up to read. And He was handed the book of the prophet Isaiah. And when He had opened the book, He found the place where it was written: "The Spirit of the Lord is upon Me, because He has anointed Me to preach the gospel to the poor; He has sent Me to heal the brokenhearted, to proclaim liberty to the captives and recovery of sight to the blind, to set at liberty those who are oppressed; To proclaim the acceptable year of the Lord,' then He closed the book, and gave it back to the attendant and sat down. And the eyes of all who were in the synagogue were fixed on Him. And He began to say to them, "Today this Scripture is fulfilled in your hearing." So all bore witness to Him, and marveled at the gracious words, which proceeded out of His mouth. And they said, "Is this not Joseph's son?" Luke 4:14-22 NKJV.

What's so incredible about all of this? Jesus stopped that morning in the middle of a sentence, at a comma in the original text, and sat down. He was proclaiming that he was indeed the long awaited for Messiah and that he was fulfilling everything he had just read. If you look at the text he was reading in Isaiah 61:1-11 NKJV you can read what is written after the comma and what Jesus is destined to return to finish.

Free ride

While the army is looking for a few good men and women, God is throwing out His dragnet in the hopes of catching every man, woman and child in a net of faith. God loves His creation and has a plan to save it and His plan is not dependent upon anything that you do or think. It's a fair plan, a merciful plan that was wrought in ancient times before the foundations of the earth were formed.

One important note here, God isn't angry with us and He doesn't want to harm us but instead offers us salvation and wants to fill our lives with peace. It's a special kind of peace; it's the kind of peace that passes all understanding. It's a gift we don't deserve and could never acquire n our own. We can't even live a good enough life that would qualify us for entrance into His kingdom. Yet, out of His deep, unfailing love for us he has provided a way into his eternal presence.

So how many people has God provided for and how will they ever get to where He lives? Who could ever know the way into His glorious heavenly realm and beyond? Well, while these answers might be blowing in the wind I know where we can find them in the bible. "For God so loved the world that He gave His only begotten Son, that whoever believes in Him should not perish but have everlasting life."

So that everyone who believes in Him will have everlasting life! All are invited to come but unfortunately not all will accept this precious gift. John 3:16 NKJV.

"For God did not send His Son into the world to condemn the world, but that the world through Him might be saved." God's plan was in place before man was created and it is from His great love for us that He sent the cure for our sin sick soul! John 3:17 NKJV.

As a pastor, I'm asked very regularly what the unforgivable sin is; well the above scripture explains that it is unbelief in Jesus Christ.

"He who believes in Him is not condemned; but he who does not believe is condemned already, because he has not believed in the name of the only begotten Son of God." John 3:18 NKJV.

So on the same night that Jesus was arrested and condemned to be crucified, he instructed His disciples that He was going away to prepare a place for them and if He went away He would also come again to bring them back to His kingdom.

"Let not your heart be troubled; you believe in God, believe also in Me. In My Father's house are many mansions; if it were not so, I would have told you. I go to prepare a place for you. And if I go and prepare a place for you, I will come again and receive you to Myself; that where I am, there you may be also." John 14:1-3 NKJV.

Now, what is holding you back from receiving a gift from God? If you are struggling with substance abuse, come to God. If you struggle with alcohol, come to God. If you struggle with lust, come to God. Whatever it is that you are chained to, whatever it is that you carry around on your back, give it to God. While twelve steps will work, why not use the one step program and give it to God?

"Come to Me, all you who labor and are heavy laden, and I will give you rest. Take My yoke upon you and learn from Me, for I am gentle and lowly in heart, and you will find rest for your souls. For My yoke is easy and My burden is light." Matthew 11:28-30 NKJV.

Jesus is inviting us to lay our burdens down on Him and offers us a free ride into eternal life.

Now maybe you can call me simple minded, or maybe borderline ignorant, but this offer sounds too good to be true. Is there a catch? Nope, it's the real deal; God has already provided the way and the means for us to be healed from sin that separates us from a holy and righteous God.

God cares for us and wants the best for us. He wants us to live lives that are free from drama, hurt and pain. He only asks that we trust Him and walk with His spirit while He illuminates our path. He promises us a safe landing at the end if we will only abide in Him. So while the road sometimes gets rough down here and filled with pitfalls, muck and mire, Jesus invites you to travel on a much better and higher highway to heaven.

My best day ever

My perfect Sunday would start off with sleeping in until 9:30 am where I would wake without the aid of an alarm clock. Walking quickly to the closet I wouldn't have any trouble picking out something to wear while my wife prepared a breakfast of poached eggs on sourdough toast. Shortly after a leisurely commute, I would arrive at church which would be packed with sinners eagerly waiting to receive the gospel. Every need of the church was already being met by a surplus of mature Christians who were more than eager to serve God.

The sound and visuals would be in the hands of capable people who had made it to church early to get everything they needed in order. The music was provided by skillful musicians who were not drawing attention to themselves while a vast assembled choir was ready to sing praises to their God. There wouldn't be any need for volunteers to greet people because everyone coming into the church reached out to greet one another.

How many Sunday sermons do we need to hear before we get the message that God wants us to contribute, to serve and give back to others? How many fruitless arguments, discussions do we need to endure or board meetings do we need to schedule before the message gets out that we are to love one another through acts of service? Where is the community in our community of believers? What are we doing as individual churches to foster unity in and around our neighborhoods?

While it's true our work for God is not the essence of our salvation, or we would all be boasting about those things we have done, but rather it's the fruit of His labor working in us. God is doing a work in all His children through a process that is many times difficult and painful. The process of surrendering to His will takes courage, determination and requires daily sacrifice on our part. With so many distractions in our lives it's no wonder our light is not shinning as bright as it could be or even shinning at all.

So many times, as a pastor, I feel like I'm preaching to the choir. Many of us have heard the gospel, know the good news frontwards and backwards and need to move forward into service. It's safe to say that Jesus didn't waste time arguing textual interpretation with religious fanatics but instead spent much of His time walking across the street to heal a leprous person, make the lame walk and make the blind to see. He even said he didn't come to serve the wealthy or heal the healthy but rather to serve the poor and heal the sick. Do the righteous need forgiveness and repentance?

Many of our spiritual lives are like an overdrawn bank account where we have too many withdraws and not enough deposits. Our earthly bank account is growing while our heavenly account has almost nothing in it. I have never known one person who on his death bed said "I wished I had worked more overtime". There has to be joy in our journey and purpose in each step we take. Our hope has to be etched into an eternity in heaven with God while our motivation has to be living in a way that puts a smile on our Lord's face.

Sometimes, I wonder what it will really be like in heaven and if I will remember all the time, I've wasted down here on earth? Every Sunday, as stand and survey the faces starring back at me from the pulpit, I often wonder if they are going to leave with a smile, a word of encouragement, a word of knowledge or are they even receiving a promised blessing by giving back to God in the form of a weekly sacrificial monetary offering. Are people being saved from a sin sick soul, are the sick being made well, are the blind receiving sight, are the lame walking and are deaf being made to hear?

We have so little time to make a difference in this world. With so many distractions and cares adding to the burden we already carry it's no wonder we have so little energy left to keep our lamps burning. Just remember life is a vapor, it forms a temporary cloud that disappears as our days so quickly begin to speed towards eternity.

So let us make each word count and every thought be pure. Never pass up an opportunity to encourage someone or help out somewhere in the world in which we live and work. The truth is God loves us. He loves us very deeply no matter how much muck and mire we trudge through.

Through the storm

"God is still on the throne and prayer changes things!" said the voice on the radio. Harold thought about that for a moment as he drove to work. He had had a fight with his wife the night before and left the house early the next morning without saying goodbye. While cruising down the freeway Harold didn't close his eyes but connected with his Creator through a short prayer.

"Lord please soften my heart and help me to show my wife more kindness" immediately his cell phone rang. The voice on the other end of the line was that of his wife's. She had called to let him know she was sorry for last night's argument and asked for forgiveness. Harold said "No, I'm the one who should be apologizing to you!"

Cheryl had to drive downtown for a doctor's appointment and try to find a parking space three blocks away during the morning rush. She circled the block several times before praying "God please don't let me be late for my appointment" suddenly a car put on its turn signal and pulled out from the curb allowing Cheryl to signal and take advantage of the large open space.

Nick fell onto the sidewalk as he left work at Harrah's Casino. He convulsed as several people stopped to give him first aid. One woman passing by knelt down and while putting her hand on his chest said a prayer "Heavenly Father please help this poor soul. Heal him and bring him back to life"

Within seconds Nick's eyes opened wide and he sat up right as several people were shocked and frightened at what they had just witnessed. Nick asked the woman what had happened to him to him as the woman replied "Why God just performed a miracle and healed you son"

Prayer is our connection to God and His unlimited resources and potential. Unfortunately, for many of us, it is has become only a vain hope or last ditch effort. Seeking God in times of trouble should be our first response. We sometimes put too much trust in ourselves when we should take a moment to go to God in prayer.

There are three pillars to a healthy Christian life; prayer, study-meditation of God's Word and the empowerment-refilling of the Holy Spirit. These three pillars work together like the legs of a three legged stool. If you lose one leg the stool becomes out of balance and will topple over.

To keep His balance, Jesus spent time getting alone and praying to the Father. He often withdrew into the wilderness to seek out the Father's will. He also filled many hours of his life by studying the Hebrew Scriptures. The Lord modeled for us the healthy way to grow in the grace and knowledge of God.

However, it wasn't until the Holy Spirit descended upon Him that He was ready for His ministry. When John baptized Jesus in the Jordan River the scriptures say that the Holy Spirit descended upon Him and the Heavenly Father spoke "This is my Son in whom I am well pleased!"

The storms of life will continue to crash around us, over us and knock us down if we are not connected to the rock. We must spend time reading God's Word for instruction and then meditate on it. Then through our regular prayer time God can move and work on our hearts and minds.

However, it is not until the third pillar is constructed that we gain our total stability and potential as Christians. When we empty ourselves and allow God to re-fill us with His Holy Spirit then we are complete and ready to stand firm in our faith.

Picture a lighthouse that has been built out at sea along the coastline. The waves continually build and crash against the structure. As the waves grow larger more pressure and force is being exerted onto the walls. However, this lighthouse's foundation has been drilled deep into the ocean's bedrock and it is not moved by the force of the waves.

Our life in Christ is just like that. We must first be connected, attached to the firm foundation of Jesus Christ. We must then spend time studying His Word and meditating on it. Then as we withdraw to spend time alone in prayer

God can work on our lives and speak to us, communicate to us through this relationship.

However, it is not until we ask God to help us through the process of empting ourselves that we can make room for the filling of the Holy Spirit. Surviving any storm depends upon being empowered by the Holy Spirit. Our power, our victory comes from God above. He is our Rock, our firm foundation and shelter from the storm.

Being patient

"Life is change" said the elderly woman who sat across from me at the car dealership. "That's what you can count on! Life will not remain the same but is always changing."

So there I was sitting, waiting for my car to be repaired, listening to a complete stranger complain about last year's service on her car. She was nice enough alright but I really hate waiting for anything especially unwanted car service while having to sit patiently trying to think up something intelligent to say.

"I hate waiting." I thought to myself as a line from a popular movie almost compelled me to shout out "You killed my father, prepare to die!"

As I looked around the waiting room I noticed several others also nervously waiting. There was an older gentleman who had on "Farmer John" overalls without any shirt underneath, sporting a mass of hair. I tried to imagine him driving his sedan to the farm to milk the cows when he notices his check engine light is on. Making a snap decision, with no time to run home to change, he drives sixty miles to the nearest car dealership.

"Are these cars costly to repair?" I had asked timidly to the valet who grabs my keys and was preparing to take my car around back. I remembered he hesitated for a moment then turned and said "Oh, yea!" with a smile and smug voice and then just sort of chuckled as my car disappeared around the corner.

Everyone seated with me, in the waiting area, were all trying their hardest to keep it together. I imagined what the service writers and mechanics were plotting behind closed doors. Have you ever taken notice that every single service writer has the title of assistant manager on the nameplate of his kiosk?

Bored, you Google the part they said you needed and found they had doubled the actual cost on your estimate? In a panic you want to leave but realize that your car is somewhere in back in a thousand little pieces. Helplessly you stare out the service room window wondering if the "new guy" got your car.

When I was younger and a very zealous Christian, I use to pray for patients. Now that I am older and wiser I no longer ask God for that particular virtue. However God, in His unfathomable wisdom, has decided that He needs to bombard me with situations that will aid me in my developing more patience.

You know those days when all the traffic lights turn green just as you approach, you find five dollars on the ground or you receive a letter, with a check, from the IRS admitting they made a mistake on last year's filing? Unfortunately, for me lately, life has been filled with long waits at red lights, endless searches for parking spaces downtown and long waits for procedures that involve allot of unwanted poking and prodding in some very personal areas.

Several weeks ago my doctor told me I needed an MRI of my brain. Being a cynic I casually mentioned "I hope they find something" to which he immediately looked at me puzzled? "Something filling the empty space between my ears" I clarified. He smiled shook my hand and I left to go find my car. When I finally remembered where I had parked I noticed the parking meter expired and the meter maid just finishing up placing a ticket under my windshield wiper.

Two days later I found myself sitting in another waiting room watching a totally different group of people waiting. Their ages ranged from small children to older adults like me. Medical waiting rooms are much more sullen and quiet than car dealerships. Here they charge even larger sums of money for their services so you had better have health insurance or you will soon find yourself homeless. Then they insist on making you fill out a plethora of paperwork and sign papers that state "although the test I'm about to take is safe there is always the possibility I could die."

Well, all this to say that God is teaching me patients. So as I age, God is reminding me that my life has always been in His hands and that He is still in control. He also wants me to change the way I treat the people He puts in my life. He especially wants me to be kind to elderly ladies at car dealerships. "Life is change" said the elderly woman who sat across from me at the car dealership. "That's what you can count on! Life will not remain the same but is always changing." So you better have patients.

Coffee and cranberry scones

The sun was just coming up over the mountains as a steady stream of droopy eyed customers repeatedly opened the swinging door into the coffee shop. Outside tables were being filled with various groups who were busy discussing their kid's soccer games, what they watched on TV last night or the latest gossip circulating around town. Off to one side, the Ridge Lake Christian men's group was meeting for early morning prayers and devotions. Hot coffee and cranberry scones were being devoured as fast as the waitress could haul them out. However, most folks sat motionless in their chairs gazing into an endless sea of laptops, notebooks, tablets and smart phones of all shapes, colors and sizes.

"You Know" paused one of the men from the church group to a woman sitting at a table behind him. "God loves you and has a wonderful plan for your life!"

"Yes, I'm sure your right" smiled the woman who was distracted and not desiring conversation turned back to her book.

"But I'm not sure you know the same Jesus that we do" continued the man with his line of questioning and who seemed to recognize the woman as belonging to a different spiritual fellowship located down the street from Ridge Lake Christian.

"Oh, well, I wasn't aware there was more than one Jesus?" snapped the woman politely yet with a smidgen of annoyance at the man's persistent inquisition.

Soon, pleasant conversation came to a halt, bibles slammed shut and all eyes became focused on the woman with spot-on, pin-point accuracy. Their glare was so intense, like red lasers in a laboratory experiment, that you could almost feel the heat and see a wisp of smoke rising from their target. The group of penitent older men had quickly dissolved into a vicious pack of young, hungry wolves and as the sun was rising they began to slowly circle their prey. All the men joined in the feeding frenzy that escalated into a shouting match across tables. Verses were now being hurled from memory, out of context, demanding that their own particular knowledge, theology and dogma were the only way to reach God.

As providence would have it a young Jewish rabbi, sitting nearby, closed his copy of the Torah and began blocking the men's rhetoric like a giant shield held high above one's head during a bright storm of flying night arrows.

"Anyway, we Jews would have to disagree with all of you" said the rabbi adjusting his round, spectacles up towards the bridge of his nose. "And I believe the fact that you are arguing with one another is proof that you don't know what real love is. None of you know the first thing about God and the great love that He has for His creation. You see, people don't care how much you know until they know how much you care." stammered the rabbi.

The preceding story is completely fictitious; any similarities to actual people, places or events are strictly coincidental.

Two thousand years ago, Nicodemus, a religious leader of Jesus' day, under the cover of darkness, came secretly stating the fact that God must be with the young rabbi. Jesus replied saying "Most assuredly, I say to you, unless one is born again, he cannot see the kingdom of God." John 3:5 NKJV. Jesus went on to say that just as Moses lifted up the bronze serpent in the wilderness so shall the Son of Man be lifted up; that whoever believed and trusted in Him would be saved. All one has to do, to be forgiven by God, is to look up to the cross, believe and to behold Jesus, God's One and only Son. He alone has paid our debt in full by becoming the payment for our sins and transgressions.

The questions we must all ask ourselves are: Have we really been born again? Are we truly transformed? Do we really love people? Are we ready to reach out a hand to someone in real need or are we quick to shout out "Be warm and be filled" but don't stop to render any assistance.

Maybe we are like some of the men in this story who are more concerned about being right, getting our own way and burdening others with long lists of pseudo rules and non-essential regulations. If we surrender to God, He will transform us to be like the young rabbi who stopped to show kindness and love to a total stranger.

"For by grace you have been saved through faith, and not of yourselves; it is the gift of God, not of works, lest anyone should boast. For we are His workmanship, created in Christ Jesus for good works, which God prepared beforehand that we should walk in them." Ephesians 2:8-10 NKJV.

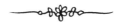

Beauty for ashes

My life, these days, I live by faith. However, it has not always been that way. I started out in life working as a carpenter building many of the homes, condos and apartments that many of you are now living in. I loved working with my hands building beautiful porticos, patios or an elegant gazebo out of a nothing but a pile of raw materials. The satisfaction that came out of cutting and assembling something out of nothing was very rewarding. To stand back and admire a structure that grew from just having an idea and a measure of faith was quite an accomplishment.

Now, I'm a pastor and live each day by my faith in God. I love the people God sends to me and get satisfaction in watching what God is building. He moves mysteriously, never doing the same thing in the exact same way. He is a master choreographer who carefully and patiently explains each step to us before we take them.

Tom and Carol had been together for twenty-five years and recently decided to get married about two and a half years ago. Last week, on Halloween, Carol began coughing and the coughing became so violent that Tom drove her into the emergency room. While Carol was being admitted to the hospital she had a massive stroke and died. What started out as a routine trip to the emergency room ended in heartbreak and loneliness leaving Tom with many unanswered questions.

While at a pastor's conference last week I received a phone call from Tom asking if I could help with Carol's "Celebration of Life" on the following Saturday. I said yes, and asked if I could pray for him. I had grown up with Tom but did not know his wife all that well. On Thursday, I called Tom to see if we could meet somewhere and discuss things. So, we met the following day and after a nice time of reminiscing I gathered a few notes and we parted company.

I love to write when God gives me ideas and they flow from my mind as fast as water running over Niagara Falls. But sometimes ideas are as scarce as rain on Southern Californian mountain sides. It's also nice to have plenty of time in order to put these words together in a way that will comfort friends and family who are gathered to remember and grieve.

While I was able to pull the main body of the service together, I still did not have the opening greeting or the closing. I went to sleep Friday night not knowing how all this was going to congeal but I had faith in God that He would give me the words to say.

As I pulled up the road there were cars lined on both sides of the curb. As I got closer to the house I still was waiting for God to give me words of comfort. With less than five minutes left, God literally gave me a section of scripture in the book of Isaiah chapter 61:1-3 NKJV, "The Spirit of the Lord is upon Me, Because the Lord has anointed Me to preach good tidings to the poor; He has sent Me to heal the brokenhearted, To proclaim liberty to the captives, And the opening of the prison to those who are bound; To proclaim the acceptable year of the Lord, And the day of vengeance of our God; To comfort all who mourn, To console those who mourn in Zion, To give beauty for ashes, The oil of joy for mourning, The garment of praise for the spirit of heaviness".

Jesus, while visiting his home town, stood up in the synagogue on the Sabbath, and read the verses recorded in Luke 4:16-21 NKJV. He stopped abruptly after quoting the verse having to do with His first coming "To proclaim the acceptable year of the Lord," Jesus stopped at "And the day of vengeance of our God." where He closed up the scrolls.

Jesus knew He was coming to the earth twice. The first time He was born to die for the sins of the world by laying down His life as a lamb led to the slaughter. The next time Jesus comes to the earth He will bring a sword of vengeance.

No matter where you are in life, no matter how lonely you are or how dark your future seems there is still hope. Jesus has come to comfort all who mourn, to give them beauty for ashes and the oil of joy for mourning. He can break those chains that bind you and open doors that have you imprisoned. He is the giver of life and invites you to partake in the Living Water. He has come to heal the broken hearted!

Beyond time

There are four basic questions that every human being will wrestle with at some point in their life. Who am I? Where did I come from? Why am I here? Where will I go when I die? I remember as a teenager thinking about these questions, including the thought of my own death, which would bring on an anxiety attack. It was freighting to realize that someday

I would cease to exist and that my consciousness would evaporate forever. Now, with all my gray hair and wisdom and thanks to my faith in God, I do not feel the same way but look forward to eternity and getting back to the future!

These four basic questions eventually lead us to only two possible world views; that everything is a cosmic accident or that we are the result of a deliberate design by a designer. For most of us, growing up in the 1960's, we were taught that outer space was infinite. We were also instructed that the microscopic world existed in an infinitely smaller and smaller direction. We were systematically taught that everything around us was the result of a cataclysmic accident. We were forced to swallow "The big bang" theory, which simply stated explains that "First there was nothing and then it blew up!" Doesn't it take more faith to believe that then in an omnipotent Creator?

So now science has discovered that our universe is not infinite but finite. They have discovered that the velocity of light is not constant but is indeed slowing down and if you have lived here on earth for any length of time it soon becomes clear that all matter goes from a higher energy state of order to a lower, cooler disorganized state. Just open your garage door (if you can) and see if it looks organized or cluttered. If left on its own does your garage contents tend to become more organized making room for the family car? As we near death even our own body begins to break down ending in one of our own major organ failure. Even our sun and the galaxy in which it resides will one day suffer catastrophic heat loss as it cools beyond a pre-determined threshold point.

So if there is a God is He getting older with us? Is His hair turning gray as He sits waiting for us to return to the garden? The answer to that question is really the one that got my attention. Since we live in three dimensional space consisting of height, length and width we can discern the fourth dimension, time, but all additional dimensions are simply just out of our ability to comprehend.

Eternity is not a place where there is an abundance of time but rather it is outside the confines of our physical universe altogether. If all of us could accept this, then most theological disputes evaporate into thin air. Here's a crude analogy: Your sitting on the main street of a metropolitan city watching a parade as it turns the corner. You can't see the beginning or the end but only the present as it rolls by you. Now think about someone sitting in a helicopter hovering over the parade route. From their perspective they can observe the entire parade at once. Every detail from the staging area, street routes as well as the finish area is observable to someone in the next dimension.

As we study the bible we find many examples of where information has been recorded ahead of time with precise detail. It's this amazing property of the scriptures that has convinced many people of the existence of God. Proof for many that the universe we are presently living in was created by an omnipotent, omniscient, omnipresent Designer.

We were not created to live like we do now, with death always looming over us. We were originally designed to live and walk with God in eternity. It was because of man's sin that God planned for his redemption from before the foundations of the world were formed. He then inspired men through inspiration by the Holy Spirit to write the bible. It is through His Word, Jesus Christ, which all creation was originally created and it is through Jesus that all men have been redeemed. All we have to do is accept this free gift God offers to us. God never forces us to do anything therefore we must turn to Him and choose to receive His forgiveness.

So, if you don't yet believe, why not take this time to ask God to reveal Himself to you personally? All you have to do is ask. Our hardware will wear out someday but our software or soul will continue to exist. So the question is where do you want to spend eternity?

Living water

Life, it's everywhere. From the lowest depths of our great oceans to the outer limits of our atmosphere life is present, adapting and growing. Look around you and you'll find water at the heart of the phenomenon. It's the medium required for life to germinate, grow and in which it flourishes. Even a tiny baby is protected and begins life surrounded by a watery bubble safe and sound in their mother's womb.

In nature water is the only compound that can exist in all three phases on earth at the same time. Our vast oceans that cover the globe surrounding continents become a giant buffering system for all life on earth. We watch and admire as water vapor is lifted from the ocean into our atmosphere forming feathery canyons and ice cream shaped castle shaped clouds. These heavy laden giants release their bounty of fresh water onto land masses where they rain soaking the ground eventually filling our rivers and streams.

All you have to do is look through a microscope at a drop of pond water to discover it teaming with life. Our planet is an amazing incubator in which all life wants to thrive and compete for its place in our world. As all living things compete for their place to survive we marvel at their apparent connection to one another.

Many cultures have searched for immortality through water. They searched far and wide traveling up mighty rivers to their source hoping to find a sacred spring or fountain that might preserve them in the hope of fighting off the inevitable aging process that brings an end to all life.

On a practical level there is nothing more satisfying to quench thirst then a glass of water. Clean, cool crystal clear water the essence of life s what your body needs and is what makes up 90 some percent of your body's mass. It is the quintessential element of all life.

Although we are mostly made of H2O there is something more that makes us who we are. It's an elusive unique quality that makes Peter different from John or James. Although it can be acquired it also seems to be pre disposed at conception through the traits carefully recorded in our DNA.

Who we are, the way in which we see the world around us as well as interact with it transcends the physical world of molecules, elements and compounds. There's an elusive spark to life that is hard to put a finger on, which can't be ignored and is present in all living things to one degree or another.

This breath of life that fills us and animates us is responsible for turning ordinary inorganic dust into living breathing creatures.

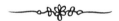

Bumper stickers

Watching bumper stickers go by can be interesting, humorous, mystifying as well as baffling. It seems many of us have the need to enlighten our fellow travelers about an idea, boast of some successful challenge or reprimand thousands of complete strangers about some pet peeve that haunts and taunts them. Some bumper stickers often reflect rude pornographic thoughts while others try and convince us that they are part of a special group, set apart for a Divine purpose.

I have often thought of several slogans myself that I believed should appear on a bumper sticker. At the time of conception they seemed like just the right message to display and that if I pursued their publication I would soon sell millions. However, after passing a work truck the other day and reading several prominently displayed bumper stickers that made absolutely no sense to me I have decided not to publish any of my own.

Some bumper stickers which encourage slower drivers to use the right hand lanes, encourage faster drivers to slow down or discourage tailgating seem to be ignored by all who need to change that specific behavior. Other bumper stickers that endorse political candidates, environmental concerns or medical cures seem like a good idea as long as they don't invite mischief from others of opposing views. We should all be willing to agree to disagree without any retaliation or resentment.

Freedom of speech, the sharing of ideas and the right to persuade others is a glorious right that is worth fighting for. Unfortunately, not everything is benign to share for discussion, publication or for our view on a passing bumper. There is a line to what is edifying and what is destructive.

One bumper sticker suggests that we should all be tolerant of each other's religious views. But what if your religious view insists on my extermination? Even within Christendom there have arisen many divisions on doctrine, tradition and religious practices. These divisions have widened so much that over the centuries many killings and bloody wars have been fought in the name of God.

Over these many centuries since the death of Jesus, the giving of the Spirit and the birth of the church divisions have continued over interpretation of what Jesus said, taught or commanded. In some instances these divisions have grown into hateful dogma that is contradictory to what Jesus originally came to teach us about; that we should love one another.

As men become more rigid and lose their flexibility their hearing begins to dim and suddenly "our way" is the only way to find God, obtain salvation or enter into fellowship with one another. Soon their causes turn to crusades that usually end with men and women were being burned, tortured or murdered.

Look around you and you will see a variety of skin colors, cultures and customs. Everyone ever born was created in the image of God. We are all His creation and children who when injured all bleed the exact same red blood. There isn't any one group that is better, has more potential or is worthy to receive special revelation.

There is a spiritual battle raging among the nations, a battle whose roots go back so far that many don't even know what it is all about. This destructive force is alive and raging on many city streets in our great country. It wasn't all that long ago that our great civil war divided families and put some brothers and cousins on opposite sides of a rifle barrel.

By definition there can only be one God and His name is Jehovah. There is only one church and Jesus is the head of it. We are all His purchased possession, His bride and bond servants who need to stop fighting and begin to allow the Spirit to do His job of cleansing us.

From the burning bush to a manger in Bethlehem God has touched the soil where we live, walked among us and has invited us to join him on a walk into eternity. The battle that rages on in the heavens among the angelic creatures doesn't have to pour out onto us here on earth to reign in our hearts and minds.

Jesus holds the key to life everlasting and He alone is the only one who is worthy to open the seal. He is the head of the church, the Alpha and the Omega. He is the bright Morning Star, first born of all creation and He will one day rule and reign, His kingdom here on earth, with an iron scepter. So If you have faith in Him then you already have His mark on your forehead. It's a mark that was made with a permanent marker, a heavenly bumper sticker that reads "I belong to Jesus!"

Carrie

Carrie was born with several genetic childhood diseases. She was the middle child in a family who were trying to make their way in a new place, the state of Oregon. She was like any other child growing up and loved to play inside with her little ponies. Carrie also loved to play with her older sister and younger brother outside in the fresh Oregon air as often as the rain and snow would allow it.

As she grew childhood epilepsy choked out many activities that other children routinely enjoyed while growing up. Carrie couldn't run around like the other kids and often had to endure whole afternoons just sitting in the house staring out the window watching other neighborhood children laughing and having fun.

School was a challenge too because the drugs she had to take for epilepsy caused her to lose focus, attention span and made her drowsy. Childhood depression soon set in as she began to withdraw from life that continued to thrive everywhere around her. To counter balance her depression she started self medicating with drugs, alcohol and tobacco.

It wasn't long before Carrie started to hear other voices in her head. The voices grew louder and louder as her substance abuse grew into a full blown addiction and she was soon diagnosed with schizophrenia. She would have to endure this paralyzing mental fragmentation for the rest of her life.

Unable to cope with the stress most people have to deal on a day to day basis, Carrie ended up living on the street where she was abused. The world is a cold, dark reality for many who are mentally or physically challenged.

Because of an ill managed and out-of-control welfare system combined with state and federal support drying up, many people who need to be institutionally taken care end up living out on our streets. Once on the streets they are forced to endure lack of nutrition, restroom facilities, and medical services while continually being battered by the harsh elements that eventually lead to premature death or incarceration.

Although many law enforcement officers try their best to help these people out, they are not equipped with the right tools or training to safely handle many situations that often turn deadly for the mentally disabled.

For Carrie her relatives were successful in finding her help which included medical, dental, a place to live and a care giver. However most people are not as lucky as Carrie and come to a tragic end while living on the street.

Carrie died yesterday at the age of thirty-nine. She went to bed and never woke up. She never really had a chance at living a normal life in this world. My only hope for her is that God in his great mercy will resurrect her in heaven and give her a new body and mind that is perfect, free from disease, where she can finally experience life as it was meant to be.

Some might call me naïve that I believe in God and know that He has a special plan for children like Carrie who are forced to grow up in a world that is fragmented and constantly coming apart at the seams. While our bodies will one day decay and turn to dust, our spirits will live on and for Carrie, well; she is finally free from the constant torture of a broken mind.

There is hope for Carrie and people like her. Actually there is hope for all people born into this world. Through God's love and mercy He planned a way that we can return back to Him. It is through the sacrifice of God's One and only Son, Jesus Christ that we can once again be healed and stand in God's presence. Jesus promised that He would prepare a place called heaven for us.

In contrast heaven will be a fresh start for us where God will wipe away every tear. In this next stop this fallen world's sin won't be a problem anymore. God will correct the destructive forces of man's will and impose His own perfect will for all eternity.

On that day the lion will lay down with the lamb while greed, selfishness and evil will be thrown into the pit of hell where they belong. What the world needs now is love. Love is only of God and not from man. We can only love because God first loved us and allows us to love through the power of His Holy Spirit.

So it is time for all of us to get together and start loving one another before our King returns for us. Again, what the world needs now is love sweet love that is the only thing that will heal the wounds of this world.

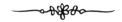

End of the rope

I went up to my room, kicked off my boots, lay down on my bed just thinking back on all the day's events. The next sound I heard was my alarm going off. I remember first hearing a very faint sound and thinking how much it sounded like my phone's alarm but that was impossible!

You see, I was twenty-five miles up in the Himalayan Mountains where I had just crossed a glacier on the south face of Lhotse. I was the lead climber on a very technical section of a route on the world's largest exposed rock face thousands of feet above the frozen ice. I could hear my phone's alarm going off even though the wind was really howling. There was only another twenty-five feet to climb before I could set up a belay station and haul up my three friends. We were in a storm, in the middle of a whiteout as the wind began to blow so hard that all I could see was ten feet of purple kern-mantel rope disappearing below me.

There is was again, my alarm, but it wasn't coming from any of the pockets on my parka. I was sure I had left my phone back at base camp with the rest of my personal belongings. The sound grew louder and louder as I fixed the last of four pitons for the belay point. I clipped in my harness and gave the rope three tugs which was the signal for the other climbers to start up. The rope tightened and stretched as the first climber's weight pulled on the pitons I had driven deep into cracks in the rock.

After a few minutes the rope stretched taut as if there were two climbers on the rope at the same time. The sound kept ringing as I tried to concentrate on handling the rope as I watched the pitons which had started bending under the additional weight. I tried to push the noise out of my head as the rope tightened again. I knew for sure something had gone wrong. Under these extreme conditions my signal had been over looked. The other climbers in a panic had begun to climb up together.

Seconds later the lowest piton began pulling out and I was instantly saturated in fear. I watched in horror as the titanium piton pull out completely and dangled loosely, clanking against the rock face. Now the number two piton was bending, starting to pull out when I heard the alarm ringing so loudly that I couldn't think what to do next. I reasoned if the second belay point pulled out I would have to be prepared to cut the rope or the last two placements would zipper out and we would all fall to our deaths but I had no way to communicate this to the other climbers. Just then the second piton shot out like a missile and the remaining two were about to do the same as I reached for my Swiss army knife.

My glove was frozen to my parka, as it broke loose it fell down out of sight just as the third placement began to come loose. I struggled to open the blade on my knife. The last two pitons exploded from the rock as I was whipped out into thin air. I was thinking that head would probably hit some rock and I'd be killed before hitting bottom. Suddenly my body slammed into something but I was still conscious alive but I wasn't cold or in a storm but looking eye to eye with a large dust bunny. In the dim light I could see the box platform of the hotel's bed and a strip of filthy carpet surrounding it.

Disorientated I got up off the floor and found my phone that I had placed on its' charger near the bed. I turned off the alarm that had been ringing for what seemed thirty minutes but in reality was probably only a few seconds. Still shaken, I had this very real feeling of joy that I hadn't had to cut my friends off the rope. Turning on the bathroom light I climbed into a very warm shower and got myself cleaned up. I was relieved that it was only a dream and that here I was, in Oregon, preparing to spend all day Sunday with my daughter and grandson.

What will you do when you get to the end of your rope? What if there isn't another incarnation waiting for you to relive? What if it isn't a dream and you wake up safe in your own room? What if you only get one chance, a choice to believe in and receive God's free gift of salvation; His One and only Son Jesus Christ.

Distractions

For some unknown reason as I looked into the mirror that sat flat on the kitchen table I began to think of impossible things. Can God make a rock so big that He can't lift it, how many angels can dance on the head of a pin and if God created other life in this universe, did Jesus have to die for them too?

Now with my mind firmly in drive and beginning to pick up momentum I surveyed other things that occupied the table around the mirror. Towards the other end a good sized pile of bills towered up, stacked one on top of the other, like a giant skyscraper. Hanging limp over the scalloped edges of a blue glass vase a handful of cut flowers. The once perky fresh flowers now cried out for mercy begging to be laid to rest on the compost pile.

On the opposite end of the table was an open calendar. Looking over the page with several dates circled I began to wonder how it could be Memorial Day already. Perspiration began to form on my forehead as thoughts of another future tax season filled my already anxious mind. Panic began to grip me and as I tried desperately to push those thoughts away I noticed how crumpled, knobby and twisted my fingers had become and began to wish that time could be put into reverse for few years.

Light from a nearby window found the mirror that was sitting on the table and directed a bright circle of light to fall upon the wall as a great witness to the Sun's power. The sun spot illuminated a portion of one wall in my house creating a perfect circle complete with crisp edges. I found myself starring back into the mirror where my mind adventure had first taken flight and then to my bible that was sitting close by.

Distractions are not a rare commodity in our lives. They proliferate and grow like the clover and dandelions growing all over our front lawns. If left unchecked they will continue to spread until they completely choke out the really important components of our lives, like our relationships to family and friends.

Like flavors of ice cream distractions can come in all shapes and sizes. We can be so distracted by work, school, projects and other life clutter that we lose sight of the light that we are suppose to be reflecting. Just as the mirror reflected the sun's bright warmth and light onto a dark corner wall in my house we too need to reflect light into the dark corners of the world we live in.

"You are the light of the world. A city that is set on a hill cannot be hidden. Nor do they light a lamp and put it under a basket, but on a lamp stand, and it gives light to all who are in the house. Let your light so shine before men, that they may see your good works and glorify your Father in heaven." Matthew 5:13 NKJV.

Being a Christian means that you not only a follower of Christ, a little Christ, but that you are a witness of Christ and should be reflecting His light, His image and His love to the people around you. Being a witness means to reflect an image of something or someone.

So as our distractions increase and we begin to lose focus on our relationship with our Creator, stop and take time to be refreshed by simply remembering who He is. God is the same yesterday, today and tomorrow and by that definition He never changes or breaks a promise He's made.

So are there things God can't do? He can't learn anything new, He can't break a promise and He will never lose anyone who has made their choice to put their faith in Him or His work of salvation.

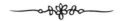

Goliath's brothers

It's the little things in the bible, that as you look at them under a greater light, give you some incredible insights. It might be a certain number used or a name; it might be even as small and seemly insignificant as a date but, rest assured, every single letter and punctuation mark are inspired by God written by men under inspiration of the Holy Spirit.

An example of this is found in the life of David in the days when he was still tending to his father's sheep. In the hills surrounding Bethlehem, David would watch over his father's flocks. Healthy sheep, left alone without a good shepherd to tend them, are easy pickings for the lion, bear, wolf or coyote. Any predator can finish off a lame animal that has fallen behind if the animal is left unguarded.

It was during this time of David's life that he went to visit three of his brothers who were fighting on the front lines about thirty miles away. The armies of both Israel and the Philistines were encamped opposite each other in the Valley of Elah. The champion of the Philistines was a giant named Goliath who was from Gath. He stood nine feet tall and was a daunting figure as he stood every morning and evening taunting the army of Israel.

As the story goes in 1 Samuel 17:40-51 NKJV, all the men of Israel were greatly afraid to go out and fight one on one with Goliath. So for forty days and nights, Israel had to endure the humiliation that was inflicted upon them by this giant; that is, until David came to visit his brothers.

David, with his sling in his hand, chooses five smooth stones from the brook. He carefully places them into his leather shepherd's bag slung around his waist. The text says that David ran towards the army to meet the Philistine. Reaching into his bag he pulled out one of the five smooth stones.

With one relaxed, incredible aim with his sling David hurls the projectile into the forehead of the giant causing him to fall to the ground. David had confidently just said to everyone present "This day the Lord will deliver you into my hand; for the battle is the Lord's and he will give you into our hands."

It's clear from the text that David was confident God would win his match with the giant Goliath. He was also well prepared at using his sling which he had used many times before as a shepherd. But the question that burns in my mind is why did he carefully choose five smooth stones from that brook?

The answer to that question can be found in 2 Samuel 21:15-22 NKJV. The text mentions that Goliath had four other brothers that were born to a giant living in Gath. So David had picked up four extra smooth stones from the brook just in case one of Goliath's four other brothers came looking for him.

So what giants are there in your own life? Do you have the same confidence in God that David had as he stood and faced the giant Goliath? Are you prepared for the battle as the giant shows up in your valley, to taunt you, trying to wreak havoc in your life?

Know this first and foremost, that when Jesus died on the cross, He said "It is finished" and the veil was torn from the top down to the bottom. This carpenter-king has paid our debt in full allowing us to once again become sons and daughters of God inheriting eternal life that was prepared for us from before the foundations of the earth were laid.

There is nothing left to fear in this life. The sting of death has been taken away for all time. This redemption is awaiting you. You can't work for it, you can't buy it, you can't be good enough to earn it but you must ask in order to receive it from the Lord! Won't you ask Him to forgive you right now?

So with confidence you too can trust that the battles you fight belong to the Lord. Remember that Jesus Christ, who said He is the Good Shepherd and will lay down His life for His sheep, is always on the alert for that one little lost lamb.

The Good Shepherd will not only lead you, feeding you on His word, but will also guide you safely to the fountain of living water that flows from the Father's throne. In this life there will be giants to run up against; there will be trails and tribulation and pitfalls to stumble into but be of good cheer because Jesus Christ has overcome the world and this present darkness.

Memorial stones

The sight of the nation of Israel camped on the east side of the Jordan River, numbering two million strong, must have been an awesome sight to behold. It would have naturally sown fear into the hearts of the inhabitants of Canaan as they watched this horde of men, women, children and their livestock cross over the Jordan River on dry ground. God was preparing to exalt Joshua in the sight of all Israel as he instructs him to command a man from each of the twelve tribes to take up a large stone from the middle of the Jordan River and shoulder it across to the other side.

The Lord wanted this to be a sign in the years to come, a road marker, a reminder and a memorial stone. "That this may be a sign among you when your children ask in time to come, saying, 'What do these stones mean to you?' Then you shall answer that the waters of the Jordan were cut off before the ark of the covenant of the Lord; when it crossed over the Jordan, the waters of the Jordan were cut off. And these stones shall be for a memorial to the children of Israel forever." Joshua 4:6,7 NKJV.

Let's take a minute to use this passage as our own memorial stone or marker reminding us how God, years before, had parted the great waters of the Red Sea allowing the Israelites to escape capture and drowning Pharaoh's army in its wake. And if you go back just days before that event, God instituted the first Passover celebration; where all Israelites were to sacrifice a lamb and smear the blood on their door posts and lintel. This feast too was to be another reminder of God's mighty provisions, and also as a prophetic sign for what He would ultimately do when His own Son would become The Lamb of God who takes away the sin of the world, Exodus 12:1-14 NKJV. The bible is so wonderfully written and divinely put together as we shall see once again in this great section of scripture.

God was instructing the Israelites to pick up twelve stones out of the river in order to assemble a memorial on the other side. Then, in years to come as they passed by this memorial, their children would ask them what were these stones piled for? God knew how quickly we forget Him and the wonderful miracles He performs in our lives. These stones would stand as a reminder and a monumental opportunity to teach about the goodness of God. What a priceless opportunity to be able to teach another generation about the sovereignty of God and how He is always there for us even as we wade through the very cold, deep rivers that can flood our lives from time to time.

Try to imagine a river sixty feet across and ten to fifteen feet deep that has been miraculously dammed up some seventeen miles away at the city of Adam. The crossing of such a large gathering of people just by itself would be quite a sight, but add onto it the miracle of the water being held back until the last Israelite crossed over. One interesting fact is that God inspired Joshua to include the date of this monumental river crossing in the text Joshua 4:19 NKJV, "On the tenth day of the first month". Remember back to the first Passover when God instructed them to take a lamb into their homes on the tenth day of the first month. They were celebrating the Passover as God held back the waters of the Jordan in much the same way He held back the mighty waters of the Red Sea and guided the Israelites safely through the sea on dry land.

Many Rabbis in Israel today say that "coincidence" is not a kosher word and for me there are just too many overlapping similarities in both Old and New Testaments to be coincidence. The Old Testament is a perfectly prophetic descriptive picture of the coming Messiah. God both designed these events and foretold them to us to strengthen our faith. Then, as He sees opportunity, He encourages the men to build a pile of memorial stones to teach future generations about His marvelous plan for our salvation.

His plan is so perfect that it stands the test of time, beckoning us to remember our own monuments in life when God saves us and breaks us away from our sin that holds us in perpetual bondage. So, I am encouraging you to set up twelve memorial stones in your own life and when your children ask you what they are for, you can answer that almighty God loves you so much and has set in motion a marvelous plan of redemption that He established before the foundations of the world were laid.

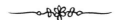

The whale is moving

Have you ever felt really alone? Like you were of no consequence to anyone or that your life was completely purposeless? Like old flavorless salt on the verge of being thrown out or a light bulb whose filament now only produces a dim glow? It's a worthless feeling of hopelessness and desperation where it seems that even God has turned his back on you.

Twenty-seven hundred years ago there was a prophet of God who was feeling like his life lacked purpose. One day God spoke to Jonah sending him to deliver a message to one of Israel's most feared and hated enemies, the Assyrians. "Arise, and go to Nineveh, that great city, and cry out against it; for their wickedness has come up before Me." But, unfortunately, Jonah disobeyed God by running away in the exact opposite direction of Nineveh.

While sleeping in the lower levels of a wooden ship that was headed for Tar Shish God sent a mighty storm to turn Jonah around. Eventually, the sailors had no choice but to throw the wayward prophet overboard which calmed the storm immediately. While Jonah is being engulfed by the sea, God prepared a great fish to swallow him. With all hope gone, while trapped in the belly of the fish Jonah cries out to the Lord for help.

It's often during these times of trial and tribulation when we remember God and cry out for His help. These dark valleys are often lonely times when we have no sensation of God in our lives; it's as if He has abandoned us. For Jonah, the belly of the fish was dank, dark, full of half eaten mackerel, plankton and reeking, rotting shark fins. Seaweed landed on his shoulders and wrapped around his neck like the regalia of a great undersea king. But make no mistake about it, the belly of the fish was a lonely place where Jonah had no sensation of movement or sense of where he was going.

Many times in my own life I have also felt lonely and abandoned by God. Usually it happens when I'm in a stressful place, when I have made some bad decisions and don't yet have the answers. The feeling of loneliness, of being abandoned by others and especially God is one of the worst places someone can find themselves.

As Jonah sat motionless in the belly of the fish, not knowing where he was headed, he took the first step and cried out to God for help. Even though the prophet was feeling like his situation was not improving the fish eventually arrived back at the place where he had started? After being deposited up on the shore, Jonah reluctantly goes to the Nineveh and completes the task God had asked him to do.

Many times in my own life I have felt alone and that the presence of God was not near me. Whether it's a family issue, work related or just feeling blue the feeling of being alone in the world is not of God. For He walks with us, and holds us up in those dark hours before the morning light begins to stream over the distant hills. He is our hope, strength and the author as well as finisher of our salvation. There is no where I can hide from His love and no where I can go to escape His presence.

God usually is busy carrying us in those times when we feel abandoned and lonely. Our faith is usually pretty weak but His grip is as strong as an infinite amount of power. He is healer; He is our friend and is not at all upset, angry or even mad at us.

"For God so loved the world that He gave His only begotten Son, that whoever believes in Him should not perish but have everlasting life." John 3:16 NKJV.

Doesn't that sounds more like a father who would do anything to save his children?

His name is salvation. He is our strong tower that we run into. We have nothing to fear for the love of God can protect us from anything evil and will break any chain that binds us. He came to set the captives free and guide us into eternity.

So remember, God is always in control, directing the man or woman of God to go in the right direction. Our destination is an eternity with our King, our Lord and our God and a guaranteed inheritance. So the next time you feel lonely or that God has abandoned you remember the story of Jonah and cry out to God, believing and trusting that He is with you knowing that the whale is moving!

Friendship evangelism

Do you have a friend? A person who is loyal to you, who would literally lay down their life for you? The only person in the world who would tell you to pick out another dress because the one you are wearing makes you look frumpy?

We were never meant to walk alone. God designed us to live as a community and set up His kingdom to operate that way. In the beginning God created a beautiful garden for us to live in and intended that we enjoy its bounty while in each other's company. He intended that we use our time and resources wisely on others around us. In fact, the relationships you make here on earth will be the only thing following you to heaven. Nobody gets to pack a u-haul trailer with all of their earthly possessions. You exit the same way you came into the world, naked!

So often our days are filled rushing around doing this and doing that. Once we complete something we cross it off our "to do" list and go onto the next item. I know I get too focused on completing the list that I fail to talk to other people along my path. Sometimes however, unavoidable situations force us to slow down and talk to each other.

Someone once said that every seat in church has a story. Some of us have lived incredible adventurous lives in our youth and have many experiences to share with one another. We need to take the time to get to know one another and enjoy the journey walking hand in hand, taking time to tell our stories. There can be joy in the journey so don't wait until it's too late, start making friends now.

For David, God would use his friendship with Jonathan to protect him from King Saul's jealous anger. King Saul was rejected by God; his anointing was removed leading the way for an evil spirit to influence him. Jonathan and David had become close friends and watched each other's back. Their friendship had allowed Jonathan to keep David informed of his father's intentions and movements as he hunted for him throughout his kingdom. Jonathan loved David and placed his own life on the line for his well-being.

When God gave the world His only Son, he gave us so much more than a Messiah-King, he gave us a friend. The very night before Jesus went to the cross He said this "These things I have spoken to you, that My joy may remain in you, and that your joy may be full. This is My commandment, that you love one another as I have loved you. Greater love has no one than this, than to lay down one's life for his friends. You are My friends if you do whatever I command you. No longer do I call you servants, for a servant does not know what his master is doing; but I have called you friends, for all things that I heard from the Father I have made known to you." John 15:11 NKJV.

So what joy is Jesus talking about if on the following morning He would be scourged, mocked and crucified? The answer is "Looking unto Jesus, the author and finisher of our faith, who for the joy set before Him endured the cross, despising the shame, and has sat down at the right hand of the throne of God." Hebrews 12:2 NKJV.

Jesus paid the original sin debt, incurred by Adam and Eve, finally nailing it to the cross for eternity. He alone provides the "Way" back to a holy, righteous Father.

Jesus spent the last three years of his life not crossing off items on His "to do" list but instead demonstrated for us how to love people. Jesus always took the time to touch someone, talk to the lonely and was always most concerned about someone's eternal destination. He often interrupted his daily schedule to touch a leper, have a meal with tax collectors and prostitutes, taking time to get to know them. He taught us what real love looks like while talking to an outcast woman at a well in Samaria. Jesus loved the journey.

Fifty days after his death, Jesus gave us the Holy Spirit as a pledge of our inheritance to come. Once filled with the Spirit of God He commanded us to go into all the world and make friends! Once we earn their respect, we can begin teaching them all the things that Jesus taught to us. Remember to take rest stops along this journey of life making friends and storing up treasure in heaven!

Twenty questions

All twenty questions listed below can be found in the NKJV if you take the time to read and study.

"He is the image of the invisible God, the firstborn over all creation. For by Him all things were created that are in heaven and that are on earth, visible and invisible, whether thrones or dominions or principalities or powers. All things were created through Him and for Him. And He is before all things, and in Him all things consist. And He is the head of the body, the church, who is the beginning, the firstborn from the dead, that in all things He may have the preeminence." Do you know Him?

"He who believes in Him is not condemned; but he who does not believe in Him is condemned already, because he has not believed in the name of the only begotten Son of God." Do you believe in Him?

"He is the Mediator of the new covenant, by means of death, for the redemption of the transgression under the first covenant, that those who are called may receive the promise of the eternal inheritance." Do you have an eternal inheritance?

"My sheep hear My voice, and I know them, and they follow Me. And I give them eternal life, and they shall never perish; neither shall anyone snatch them out of My hand." Do you know His voice?

"I have come as a light into the world, that whoever believes in Me should not abide in darkness." Do you walk in His light?

"A new commandment I give to you, that you love one another; as I have loved you, that you also love one another. By this all will know that you are My disciples, if you have love for one another." Do you show kindness and mercy to others?

"My kingdom is not of this world. If my kingdom were of this world, My servants would fight, so that I should not be delivered to the Jews; but my kingdom is not from here." Are you fighting for His kingdom?

"In Him you also trusted, after you heard the word of truth, the gospel of your salvation; in whom also, having believed, you were sealed with the Holy Spirit of promise, who is the guarantee of the purchased possession, to the praise of His glory." Are you sealed and looking forward to what we have been promised by God?

"If you abide in My word, you are My disciples indeed. And you shall know the truth, and the truth shall make you free. Therefore if the Son makes you free, you shall be free indeed" Is the light from His Son's-rise setting you free?

"If you knew the gift of God, and who it is who says to you, 'Give me a drink', you would have asked Him, and He would have given you living water." Have you come to drink from His fountain of life which overflows with living water?

"Come to Me, all you who labor and are heavy laden, and I will give you rest. Take my yoke upon you and learn from Me, for I am gentle and lowly in heart, and you will find rest for your souls. For My yoke is easy and My burden is light." Have you taken a step to lay your burdens at His feet?

"Therefore whoever confesses Me before men, him I will also confess before My Father who is in heaven. But whoever denies Me before men, him I will also deny before My Father who is in heaven." Have you told anyone about Him?

"Most assuredly, I say to you, unless one is born again, he cannot see the kingdom of God. That which is born of the flesh is flesh, and that which is born of the Spirit is spirit." Have you been born again spiritually?

"I am the resurrection and the life. He who believes in me, though he may die, he shall live. And whoever lives and believes in Me shall never die." Do you believe this?

"Let your hearts not be troubled; you believe in God, believe also in Me. In My Father's house are many mansions; if it were not so, I would have told you. I go to prepare a place for you. And if I go to prepare a place for you, I will come again and receive you to Myself; that where I am, there you may be also." Do you know the way?

Heaven indeed awaits us! God is calling everyone who will listen to His voice to come and drink from His living water. He calls to you. He died for you. He left the other sheep to look for you. He is a chain breaker, a promise keeper and debt forgiver. He stands at the door and knocks, will you answer? Do you know Him? His name is Jesus!

Messiah

The date the Messiah would return was set in stone, scribbled on a sacred scroll penned by the Prophet Daniel. Sent to man by God through the angel Gabriel; the day of salvation was clearly foretold to the exact day. The Scribes, Priests and Pharisees had memorized the words, calculated the date but were still blinded, unable to see the miracle God was performing.

From the very beginning of creation God only wanted to walk with man, to create in Adam the ability to choose to love Him but man turned away from his creator and followed a self-centered destructive path filled with lust, greed and power.

In time God raised up a remnant, a family clan, from Noah's son Shem. It was His plan and hope that He could reveal Himself to the entire world through the good works of this one family line. As time passed and the family grew into a nation, they too turned away from God following a destructive path of self indulgence while worshipping gods made by their own hands.

Once again out of His great love and mercy, God sent the prophets to warn His people to return to fellowship with Him but instead the nation killed the prophets and walked further down the road of bondage. Instead of being a great light to the world they became a perverted darkness, sinking lower and lower into the pit of depravity.

Finally, after seventy years of captivity, God heard the cries of His people and freed them from their servitude in Babylon. It was during this period that God sent the angel Gabriel to Daniel. He explained what would transpire in the future and how He would bring peace back to the world.

God's prophets had foreseen these two great appearances of the Messiah but from their perspective it looked like a single mountain peak on a distance horizon. They couldn't see the valley that lay between the Messiah's first and second appearances.

We are now living at a time on the furthest edge of that valley. The return of the King is imminent and when He does return He will set into motion the seventieth week that the angel Gabriel delivered to the prophet Daniel over twenty-five hundred years ago.

Who is this King of Glory? In the Greek His name is Jesus, in Hebrew Jeshua (Joshua) and He is the Alpha and the Omega or the beginning and the end. God promised that He would be the One to pay all back all debts and accomplish the work of salvation through His crucifixion in Jerusalem.

After dying, Jesus returned from death and promised new, eternal life to all who would only believe and put their faith in Him. Then He went away to prepare a place for His bride "the church" promising one day to return for us.

It is this event that we are expectantly waiting for and warned will take place in the twinkling of an eye right before the seventieth week or the seven year period know as the day of "Jacob's trouble".

God doesn't want our religion. He made it clear that we have no part in salvation and that it is in Him and Him alone that we are saved from evil. Even the earth is in bondage and groans while it awaits its freedom and restoration. The seventieth week is about to begin and will usher in the second appearance of Jesus Christ who will at that time set up His kingdom here on earth.

The earth is about to enter its sabbatical rest of one thousand years which is referred to as the Millennial Kingdom. At that time, Jesus will rule and reign this kingdom with an iron scepter and there will be peace on the earth.

God doesn't want man's religion, filled with endless rules and regulations; all He wants from us is a relationship where we chose to walk closely with Him in love. The law can only bring us to the edge of the Promised Land, it cannot lead you in. The only way into the Promised Land is by following Joshua (Jeshua in Hebrew, Jesus in Greek).

When Martha and Mary's brother died Jesus told them that he would live again. He went on to explain that He was the resurrection and the life and that anyone who believed in Him would never die. He also explained to the apostles that He was the only Way, the Truth and the Life and that anyone desiring to tabernacle with God could only approach through Him.

This present world is running on greed; money has become the god of our world system. When Jesus returns to set up His kingdom it will be love that prevails and motivates us to good works.

Turn, turn, turn

As I am getting older there seems to be more funerals and memorials being scheduled in my life "Turn, turn, turn". I don't like it when I get the news that someone I knew, who is younger than I am and in perfect health at the time, succumbs to a stroke "Turn, turn, turn". I would much rather hear about the twins that were born on New Year's eve to my neighbors down the street "Turn, turn, turn". Then watching from a distance as the paint is being thrown up on the walls of the newly converted kid's nursery it makes me happy to reflect back on the new beginnings in my own life "Turn, turn, turn".

However, this big old globe we live upon continues to turn causing the winds to blow and our children's feet to stay planted firmly on its rich vibrant soils "Turn, turn, turn". Our kids continue to run and jump, with string in hand, chasing after the wind as a stubby tailless kite is being dragged along usually upside down and nowhere near to taking flight "Turn, turn, turn". However, as I struggle to my feet against constant complaints from my knees, I hear the winds outside making the rafters and beams of my home creak and moan "Turn, turn, turn".

The recent rains have brought with them much relief from the scorching drought reviving old growth and bringing new life to many volunteers in my garden "Turn, turn, turn". The thought of having to cut down all the weeds that are beginning to push through the soil makes me shiver, weep and reminds me not to make any plans for the next three months of weekends "Turn, turn, turn". Looking down I laugh at my index finger which is about half healed from a renegade broken chain on my saw "Turn, turn, turn".

From a random pocket dial I hear a friend from his hospital bed crying out in intense pain, then at the same time a text pops up from another friend who announces that her cancer scan has come back cancer free "Turn, turn, turn". Standing next to the lake I pick up five smooth, flat stones and skip one of them seven times across the glass like surface "Turn, turn, turn". Later that day I stop to help a friend gather large stones from a field where we set them into wet mortar for his home's foundation "Turn, turn, turn".

Once back at home I frantically search for my phone, which has become a frequent night time task, finding it hidden under the cushion of a chair I wonder why I have let myself become so dependent on it "Turn, turn, turn". I read an article, in my local paper, which says that the government would like to begin inserting chips under the epidermal layer of our right hands in an attempt to scuttle credit card fraud "Turn, turn, turn".

On the home front our rockets have long silenced their boosters from our indoor basketball courts as chargers prepare to mount a complete full scale retreat to their final resting place in Los Angeles "Turn, turn, turn". Many popular movies vie for our attention from Hollywood's silver screen as sixty inch flat screens continue to drop in price amid Black Friday's din. "Turn, turn, turn". Caught up in all the entertainment there is little time left for prayer, Wednesday night 7:00 pm bible study at our Youth Center or Sunday morning 10 am service at our local church where people encourage, exchange stories and embrace one another "Turn, turn, turn".

As I survey my packed closet I realize that two thirds of the clothes are not being worn anymore and begin to think about what it would be like to de-clutter my closet as well as my life "Turn, turn, turn". So while I'm out getting boxes to throw away all articles I no longer want, I stop and look through the clothes racks at my favorite discount clothing store where I pick out eight items I just can't live without "Turn, turn, turn". As I'm leaving I try and rush threw the automatic swinging doors as they are closing and catch my flannel shirt on the handle putting a huge tear down the back "Turn, turn, turn". I stop and change into a new shirt I have just purchased and drop off my torn shirt at the tailor's shop located near where I am parked, where he insists he will have no trouble sewing up the rip "Turn, turn, turn".

All our fruitless struggles, our endless worries won't travel with us when we cross the great veil that separates us from our Heavenly Father. Everything is vanity; except for our relationship with Christ!

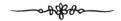

Shipwrecked

Paul left Caesarea in chains with one hundred and twenty-five other prisoners. The storm season was approaching as the hot summer temperatures had vanished allowing cooler air to flow into the area from the north. As they boarded the tall wooden ship bound for Italy the captain knew they would be sailing on the cusp of possible bad weather. With a crew of fifty and one hundred Roman soldiers aboard the total human compliment was two hundred and seventy-five.

The ships manifest also listed hundreds of flagons of olive oil, wine and wheat which made the ship's draft ride low in the water. Julius was the centurion in charge of getting Paul and the other prisoners safely to Rome. Many of them would have to endure weeks of heavy ocean travel only to end up as food for the hungry lions in the coliseum.

Julius was a middle-aged Roman centurion who was in charge of getting Paul and the rest of the prisoners to Rome. He had taken a liking to Paul allowing him to leave the ship in Sidon to visit with a group of Christian friends. Julius, when he was a younger man, had been part of the regiment that had crucified Jesus Christ along with two other prisoners in Jerusalem. It was on that day when Jesus was crucified that the young Roman soldier had a small seed of faith planted and started to believe in the God of Abraham, Isaac and Jacob.

The wind was pushing against them and sailing was slow as they headed up to Myra to find a larger ship that could make the trip to Italy. That night Paul had a premonition that the voyage would end in disaster and on the next morning tried to convince the Centurion, the helmsman and the ship's owner to winter in the harbor. However, a delay would mean less profit for the ship's owner so pressure was applied and the Centurion decided to leave the harbor and sail for the Italian coast.

Soon the situation worsened as Paul predicted and the heavy ship began taking on water as rough seas poured over the ship's railings and onto the deck. The prisoners were compelled to handle the bilge pit and bucket out the water that flowed continually into it. The sailors too were busy lightening the ship by throwing all un-nessacerry goods overboard. They ran cables and ropes under the ship to hold it together from the constant pounding of the fierce ocean waves. On the next day, fearing the worst, the crew began throwing the ship's tackle overboard.

Julius had remembered Paul's prediction and believed it was the God he worshiped that had sent him the vision. For fourteen days the tempest blew the rain sideways and all on board could neither see the sun or stars as hope flickered like the wick of a candle that had used up all of its wax? The crew had all but given up any hope of surviving the dark night as the soldiers prepared to execute all the prisoners. Several sailors began lowering the only life boat into the water.

Paul boldly informed the Centurion about an angelic visit that night and that God was going to spare everyone's life if they would all just stay on board the ship. Immediately Julius barked out orders to cut the ropes holding the lifeboat and stopped the soldiers from harming the prisoners. At daybreak the ship ran aground on a reef and was beginning to break up as the waves pounded from behind. Those that could swim were told to make for the shore followed by everyone else who was clinging to barrels, wooden planks and anything that would float. They all made it safely to land.

It's often in our pitch black, wave swollen lives, in the midst of the storm, that we call out to the Lord for help and begin to cling to Him. It's often in our darkest hours, before the dawn, when we feel our situation is hopeless that we feel God's presence the most. While he doesn't promise us life without storms He does promise to walk with us through the very heart of our crisis.

In Paul's story the sailors weren't taken out of their circumstances but were given hope and encouragement through the storm to persevere. God used Paul, one faithful God believing person, to influence the Centurion who immediately stopped the sailors from leaving the ship which would have meant their certain doom.

While we might have to do a little swimming, board surfing or barrel riding in this life; God will guide us into safe harbor. Our final destination, our safe harbor, lies ahead of us across this horizon beyond time and space into eternity with our Creator.

The potter's house

We had just arrived for a long awaited family reunion and huddle at a very secluded Christian camp located in a remote area of the Santa Cruz Mountains. Small contingents of my wife's family, fifty-five in all was just getting out of their cars and were busy hugging and shaking hands. The Santa Cruz Mountains are beautifully placed between the beach town of Santa Cruz and the major metropolitan area of San Jose, California. A gentle westerly was blowing and everything in bloom was sending out fragrances of spring into the air.

The camp staff had just finished preparing a wonderful meal for us to enjoy. A large brass bell was being rung calling us to the dining room to eat as camp workers were busy setting up tables. The staff was all part of a program that helps men and women get off the streets, drugs, alcohol and sexual additions. As I walked through the buffet line each food tray was manned by someone from the program who graciously heaped food onto our plates. It wasn't the food but their pleasant faces and their smiles that caught my attention.

These were not the expressionless faces of bored, disgruntled employees but the shining faces of joyful bond servants that had been set free from bondage and were truly grateful to be serving us dinner at the camp. They were laboring as unto the Lord and their sincerity and love poured out on us like butterscotch and stuck to all our senses. It was good to see the Lord working in the lives of these young men and women from a local youth ministry and how God had His hands on them actively molding their lives.

The scene made me think how our Lord has put such a great treasure into these plain earthen vessels. It made me consider going down to the potter's house and watch as he created some of his wares on the wheel. Soon my feet were heading down the hill and within minutes I arrived at the workshop's white picket fence, unlocked the gate and stepped quietly into the potter's studio.

In the afternoon sunlight I stood silently and watched the potter clasped his hands around a lump of clay that was spinning on the wheel. He pulled and pushed on it up and down a few times as the clay went round and round the wheel. At the right moment, he put his thumb into the middle of the lump and began forming a hole. Within seconds the hole enlarged and transformed the lump into a beautiful vessel.

Unfortunately, as the lump turned a small imperfection made a large bulge in the wall of the vessel. It looked almost perfect except for the bump that now wobbled. The clay continued to bump and thump each time it went around the wheel as it hit the potter's knuckle. Soon it weakened and collapsed and the beautiful vessel was now a broken and worthless mass of clay unable to hold anything.

Determined the potter gathered up all the clay and put it back into a ball. Skillfully he applied just the right amount of pressure to the lump re-centering it on the spinning wheel. Now, with the imperfection taken away the lump was allowed to spin free. Soon the wheel stopped turning, and within a few weeks the vessel was fired, glazed and is now holding olive oil in the camp's kitchen.

In the above illustration, we are the clay, God is the Potter and the wheel represents our lives with all of its challenges, circumstances, trials and tribulations. We all have imperfections that cause our vessels to be out-of-balance. Our vessels are often cracked pots that are unable to hold anything. Its only when we ask God, the Master Potter, to intervene in our lives that He is able to take a broken, marred lump of clay and turn it back into a beautiful solid vessel.

Once we become vitrified, through the intense heat of life's fire, we are now able to hold oil. The oil is symbolic of the Holy Spirit. God wants desperately to use us as vessels of honor which are set apart for only His use. His desire for our lives is that we continually ask Him to be re-filled with the oil of the Holy Spirit.

As I looked at all the friendly faces of the workers serving us food at the camp I realized how they all had at one time been broken, worthless lumps of clay. However, God in His limitless grace and mercy had re-created them into vessels of honor that were being used by the Master Potter to graciously pour out the gospel of eternal life on the people that they were serving.

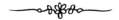

The playground

I don't remember dreaming about anything just waking up to my phone buzzing. "OK, breakfast is ready, enjoy your walk along the river David!" said Elise in her text. Her words made my mind re-trace every footstep of the night before. I had to quickly shower, throw on some clothes, grabbed a cup of coffee in the lobby and ran out the back door towards the highway that led down to the river. It was cold this morning so I was glad I had put on an extra sweater under my ski jacket. The dampness in the air penetrated my clothing and was getting right down into my bones.

I stopped halfway across the footbridge that crossed the river. It looked peaceful as it flowed over and around underwater obstacles in its path. It looked happy and made wonderful noises as it ran underneath me. There seemed to be joy in its journey that would someday lead to a wide open ocean.

The scenery was spectacular in the early morning light and reflected off the river as it flowed under the interchange. The stark lonely walk of last night had suddenly turned into a totally new experience. I passed several people walking their dogs as I crossed over the walking bridge that connects to the riding-hiking path. It was now bustling with people riding bikes, walking and several joggers sporting Nike running shoes. The walk was going quicker today as it didn't take long to cross the river, walk under the freeway overpass and into a beautiful park-like space.

The trees looked friendlier too, now that they had abandoned their black robes. In the morning light, instead of resembling bony witches' arms, they now held song birds that were busy flying back and forth between trees. The deciduous trees were all decorated with hanging moss and lichen that dangled from bare branches. Birds of all kinds were waking up with the sun busy scurrying back and forth on the ground foraging for food. Years of falling leaves had created a rich dendrite on the forest floor that was swarming with insects.

I kicked a couple of aluminum beer cans off the path as I continued my walk through this enchanting forest of mixed conifers and deciduous trees. It wasn't long before I came to a children's playground that I hadn't notice last night in the dark. It was recently installed brand new and there was an immense lawn that circled around it. The grass was just mowed giving it that freshly-cut grass smell I remember from high school football practices. Looking closely at this newly constructed play structure it was hard to imagine how it passed through the planning and building departments?

When I build new homes or renovate old ones I have to adhere to rigid safety and building codes but here on this equipment the stairs had no hand railings. They led upward to a platform three feet off the ground that had no railings. A wooden slated rope bridge swayed as the cracks between the boards were just large enough to pinch the hands and fingers of a small child. The shaky rope bridge led to another set of stairs, again with no side railings, and then climbed to a height of six feet where kids could jump off onto contorted fireman's pole. I wondered why, as a contractor, I'm not allowed to build an outdoor residential deck over 32" in height without a railing? However, these playground companies are allowed to design and manufacture play equipment for children that are an absolute safety nightmare?

As I walked, I thought about the playground design and wondered if my own life resembled the peacefully flowing river, the stately, grand landscaped forest or a chaotically designed child's playground equipment. Soon I past a bench and decided to rest. Sitting there, on the bench catching my breath, it dawned on me that it is the choices me make that place us in the situations we find ourselves in. It might be a quick irrational choice to jump up onto the bridge's protective railing that causes us to fall into the river. It could be a hasty decision to leave or get a divorce from the man or woman we married in our youth that lands us in desolation. However, many times our lives resemble the jungle gym of unsafe twisted metal in the playground as we stand dangerously close to the edge of a platform that has no railing.

Sometimes we just need a rest. We need to sit down on a bench in the park and relax away from all the hustle and bustle. Trusting that God is working in our lives is a good place to start. Let us all begin by laying our burdens down at the Jesus' feet.

Overflowing cups

I was walking towards my house with hands were full of books, groceries and a coffee cup that was full to the brim. As I tried to open the latch to the gate my coffee cup spilled out dousing all my bible study material. Life is so busy and our hands so full of things that at times can be overwhelming. But even though life's pressures were pushing down on me I was determined to see all the blessings in my life.

God's blessings were all around me as I walked past the wooden gate that leads into the courtyard where a bubbling fountain and a plethora of colorful flowers were in bloom. Even before taking a step past the front gate a chest high rose bush filled with coral colored flowers exploded in front of my eyes. The colorful roses beckoned me to come in for a closer look and fully sample their heavenly aroma. A few feet in front of me purple iris reached up from their dark green foliage seemly to smile at me with pursed lips.

All this beauty, all these fragrances, it was all so wonderful being surrounded by so many splendors that I had to vocally reach out with praises to our Great God! We all have so much to be thankful for and so often don't take the time to not only smell the roses but thank the one who made them. There are so many things, so many blessing to be thankful to God for that we should take more time to praise Him and thank Him. Too often we offer up our prayers, our "want lists" before giving our Lord the thanksgiving he deserves for all the things in life we take for granted; life, air to breathe, water to drink etc. As members of Christ's church we are told to have a wonderful aroma and beautiful fragrance that over-flows out of our lives where ever we go. In fact our fragrance should draw others to God through our example; the way in which we live and treat others. The fragrances we should be diffusing at all times are: love, joy, peace, longsuffering, kindness, goodness, faithfulness, gentleness and self control.

Unfortunately, many of us have one foot in the world and one foot climbing a heavenly ladder. Instead of edifying one another our actions end up causing us to sow seeds of strife and disunity in the body of Christ. The list that follows contains things we need to avoid at all costs: adultery, fornication, uncleanness, lewdness, idolatry, sorcery, hatred, contentions, jealousy, wrath, selfish ambitions, dissentions, heresies, envy, drunkenness and revelries.

If we look at our lives as vessels or cups it is easy to evaluate the things that we fill them with. What are we filling our cups with? Are we characterized by being drunk with wine, having out bursts of wrath or are we full of hatred, envy or jealousy? It is of the utmost importance that we do not stir up contentions or cause dissentions among the brethren.

Instead we must choose to make a conscious choice to continually ask God to refill our cups. We need Him to fill us with God's Holy Spirit which is the only way to produce Spirit grown fruits of love, joy, peace, longsuffering, kindness, goodness, faithfulness, gentleness and self control.

As we empty ourselves of our own selfish ambition God is then able to set us apart as vessels of honor. Now we are ready to be filled to overflowing with His love to the point where we are spilling out onto others around us.

It is only as we set our lives apart for God's use that He can work through us to accomplish His will. For we are His workmanship created for good works that He prepared ahead of time that we should walk in them. We are saved by His grace through faith and not of ourselves; salvation is a gift from God and not of works lest any of us should boast.

We are clothed in Christ's righteousness and not by our own works. It is Jesus' white robe that removes our nakedness, our sin from the eyes of a holy and righteous God. We are then able to come into His presence because of the work that Jesus accomplished by giving His life for us as He was nailed to a Roman cross.

So as I walked through my beautiful garden with a full cup of coffee I was reminded that I too need to be filled to the brim with all of God's goodness, grace and mercy. I need to stop and meditate giving thanks to God for all the fragrances that He diffuses through my life and for all my beautiful roses!

Portrait

The portrait hung on the north wall of the great hall. The image that was preserved was a commanding presence that filled up the ancient stone wall almost completely. It truly was a beautiful representation of a king. The artist had demonstrated incredible skill in capturing his subject's spirit on a rough canvass while only using his imagination, five colored tubes of oils and a palette knife.

The king's emotions, thoughts and feelings had been captured and transported through time miraculously surviving the sunlight's intense destructive fury. It was evident that he must have been as large in life as he now appeared on the picture that hung on the wall.

Who was this king of glory, who stood so majestically, dressed in a long white robe with a golden band around his chest? He was clutching in his arms a bewildered little lamb whose long lanky legs dangled from his grasp. The lost lamb had been rescued from a pack of hungry wolves that could still be seen lurking in the background.

I wanted to know this King, to understand why he was standing there holding that helpless little lamb. Was he some kind of shepherd-king who left his palace in search of his lost sheep? His pleasant smile called to me as I felt the need to talk to him and hear his soft caring voice.

I as stood there admiring his portrait I found myself longing to be returned through time to the day that the portrait depicted, to sit nearby, at the Master's feet, under the shade of a large tree and observe this one moment in time. I wondered if he would care for me in the same way that he held that lamb so close to his heart.

It made me consider why this king had left the lavishness of his palace to roam the hills and valleys looking for lost sheep? The robe he wore hung down to his bare feet, white and looked pure as the driven snow. His head and hair were also white and his bare skin was like glimmering bronze in the midday sunlight. He had a golden band around his chest which made him a priest. So who is this shepherd-king who was also a high priest?

I can only imagine when he spoke his voice was powerful like the sound of mighty waters. With His voice he spoke the universe into existence, raised the dead back to life and called to faithful to himself. His countenance was like the sun shining in all its glory! So bright and full of light that I couldn't even gaze at him for very long.

This kind king healed the sick too. He restored the sight of the blind, made the lame to walk and cast out demons that came to torment their victims. He was a great physician, a loving shepherd, a king and a servant to all. He promised that he would one day return for his bride and so here we wait making ourselves ready for his imminent appearance.

"Lift up your heads, O you gates! And be lifted up, you everlasting doors! And the King of glory shall come in. Who is this King of glory? The Lord strong and mighty, The Lord mighty in battle. Lift up your heads, O you gates! Lift up, you everlasting doors! And the King of glory shall come in. Who is this King of glory? The Lord of hosts, He is the King of glory." Psalm 24:10 NKJV.

So who is this King of Glory? His name is Jesus! There is no sweeter name in all the earth. The mountains tremble at His name and the seas roar at his command. He causes the sun to shine and allows moon to stay in a perfect orbit. He designed the earth to tilt, wobble bringing the four seasons for our enjoyment. He causes the rain to fall on both the righteous and the wicked.

Suddenly, I was returned back to the great hall where I had been admiring the portrait of this magnificent king.

213

Where had I gone, how long had I been absent I did not know. Slowly my consciousness returned to me and I returned my gaze to the shepherd-king hanging on the wall and remembered something about him while I was gone.

He was Joseph's son and he was born in the town in Bethlehem. He grew up in Nazareth and walked the hill country around the great inland sea of Galilee. He was born of a virgin and was the Son of God. He was without sin; his blood was pure and was not under the curse from Eden. He willingly allowed himself to be crucified so that you and I could one day be free. His name is Jesus.

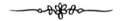

Public service

Kenny sat expressionless on the frigid chrome steel wheelchair while gazing down at the stumps that used to be his legs. He had just been released from Mercy hospital after both his legs were amputated two week ago Friday. He had been wounded after an IED exploded near him, tearing open the armored vehicle, while serving his country in Afghanistan.

Born at his hometown hospital, Kenny grew up playing kid's football in the local park. He attended the local High School and immediately following the aftermath of the terrorist attack on 911, Kenny willing joined the army. While on deployment, overseas serving his country, both his parents had been injured in a hit and run accident then taken off life support several months later.

All family assets were liquidated to pay the costly medical expenses which occurred while his parents were in the ICU.

Now homeless, hooked on prescribed pain medication, Kenny was forced to live in city parks where he had access to public restrooms. As he wheeled across the freshly cut grass he remembered much happier times when he had practiced football at the south end of the local park.

As he wheeled up to the restroom complex, he noticed that they were all locked and closed to the public. Rotten food and trash were scattered all around as it overflowed from city trash cans. Regular trash collection had been suspended and now the content in the cans was putrefying.

There were also several new signs posted around the park, stating that it was now illegal to share food with people on any city-public property. Kenny's heart broke. Tears began to fill his eyes as a police patrol car made its rounds through the parking lot. The police car stopped near the restrooms as both officers got out to investigate what Kenny was doing there.

"You can't stay here in the park" said the senior officer adjusting his pants up over his hips.

As Kenny wiped his eyes and brushed the hair away from his face the younger policeman thought he might have recognized Kenny from his army unit in Kandahar.

"Kenny? I lost track of you after the incident. Heard they transported you to Germany." said the young officer.

The senior officer pulled his partner aside to discuss the situation. Then, after several minutes of intense discussion, the younger officer explained to Kenny that his shift was almost over and that he should wait there on the sidewalk and he would pick him up for lunch in just a few minutes.

It's shameful that some people look at the homeless as just fodder that needs to be tilled under, trash to be disposed or at the very least swept under the rug. Locking public restrooms, neglecting to empty overflowing trash cans denies the public of a safe and clean place where they can relieve themselves and wash their hands with soap and water.

Passing laws that make it illegal to share food is appalling when there are men and women, just like Kenny, living out on the streets that need a helping hand. It's true that local churches have feeding programs but shouldn't our city politicians have the responsibility to help all citizens that are living within their limits?

Locking public restrooms, not removing trash and providing ill-maintained port-a-potties is a situation that may be contributing to the existing health epidemic plaguing our county and cities. Most portable toilets are not handicap accessible and, when not routinely maintained, can be a source for hepatitis A as well as many other communicable diseases.

Over two thousand years ago, Jesus warned us that we need to love people by helping them. Jesus said that we need to love others as we love ourselves. Jesus Himself both touched and hugged men and women who had leprosy. He insisted that true religion is helping widows and orphans in their distress; to reach out to the homeless, undesirables as well as the lost.

In the gospel of Matthew we find an intense judgment by Jesus on those people who refused to help others.

"Then they also will answer Him, saying, Lord, when did we see You hungry or thirsty or a stranger or naked or sick or in prison, and did not minister to You? Then He will answer them, saying, Assuredly, I say to you, inasmuch as you did not do it to one of the least of these, you did not do it to Me. And these will go away into everlasting punishment, but the righteous into eternal life." Matthew 25:44-46 NKJV.

Tin Can

The kitten darted back into the protection of an empty can of ranch beans. She was as orange as a carrot and as quick as a gazelle. Nobody knew where the little one belonged but all agreed that she couldn't be much older than five weeks. How she had survived the many hazards of Pine Springs RV Park was beyond comprehension. From the security of her new armored cave the tiny kitten hissed and swatted at anyone who tried to come close. She had already bitten a very nice lady who discovered her hiding beside her trailer partially hidden under a mountain lilac.

Before long a plan was conceived and put into action to capture the kitten and get it out of danger and into the security of someone's home. A simple cage with food was set out to lure the animal in. After several minutes, with everyone hiding just out of sight, the hungry, little orange tabby creped cautiously into the cage as the park ranger let go of the string that held up the door. The little kitten, which could have easily fit into the palm of your hand, threw back her ears, bared her sharply pointed teeth and scratched several times at the air.

A phone call was made to a local pastor's wife and within minutes she was on her way to claim the frightened animal. Jane was excited to finally have another addition to their family as they had recently lost another cat to old age.

Once arriving at their house Jane prepared the bathroom placing the kitten and cage on the floor and opened the door. The kitten quickly ran out taking up a strategic position behind the toilet where she felt safer to fend off predators.

She was wild at heart and determined to stay that way. Many attempts were made to coax her out from behind her porcelain protection using a variety of foods, kitten treats and soft singing but the little tiger would not budge and hissed threatening to bite at every attempt that was made.

Jane imagined how the little kitten must have felt being born into a crazy, dangerous world filled with a variety of metal machine monsters. These steel giants not only towered over her but made loud terrifying grinding; clicking noises that sent her scurrying back to the protection of the can. The park was located at the edge of a wild forest area where many predators like raccoons, skunks, weasels, possums, bob cats, mountain lions and coyotes randomly wandered through Pine Springs in search of unsuspecting prey. The little newborn kitten was an easy target.

Once Jane returned home she was eager to reach out to hold her new prize. She had a soft spot in her heart for small animals and without thinking quickly reached behind the toilet gently picking up the kitten. Immediately the cute little kitten transformed into a whirling dervish of fur, sharp claws and needle like teeth that pierced her flesh as she squirmed and churned in Jane's hands. When the dust finally had settled there was not one finger without a wound.

Bound and determined to pet the kitten, one of Jane's children rolled up a soft, fluffy scarf and put it on the end of a long stick. Slowly reaching back towards the kitten the friendly soft balled up scarf began gently rubbing the top of the kitten's head. At first she instinctively began to hiss and then as if a switch was turned on began to purr very loudly.

The next day a stuffed animal was introduced instead of the fluffy scarf and it wasn't long until the stick was replaced by the son's warm hand. It was amazing to see how quickly the kitten responded to the family's care, love and kindness.

Watching this entire story unfold caused me to pause and think about many people we meet in our lives as we work and wander through this world. Just like the kitten many people have grown up or are living in situations where they are not receiving enough love, kindness or encouragement to mature into healthy, well adjusted people. Children especially need to feel secure and the ones who grow up without the love of a parent often develop defensive postures for life just was the case of the little kitten that was hiding behind the toilet.

When our Lord, Jesus of Nazareth, walked the earth he poured out His entire life to love, nurture and encourage people to thrive. He reassured people that their Heavenly Father really loved them. He never missed an opportunity to reach out to anyone who needed hope. People will eventually respond to us if we will do our part to reach out to them where they are with love.

Battle plan

Moshe chopped up the cilantro, garlic and jalapenos for the salad. His style of cooking was spicy as well as a bit on the hot side. The church's kitchen was small and there was very little space for more than one cook. Sofia was a wonderful beautiful woman who had taken over the preparation of the church's fellowship dinners for the past two years. She was extremely stressed this afternoon as she kept trying to work around Moshe who had a cutting board, several sharp knives and salad fixings spread out over most of the kitchen's limited counter space.

Everyone looked forward to the Wednesday church dinner as it was always a pleasant way to spend a night worshipping God, fellowshipping with others and sharing a wonderful meal together. Moshe was new to the fellowship and wanted to help out anywhere he could. Providence had brought both cooks together this particular evening as God began to test their patients.

Preparing meals for large church crowds is what Sofia was gifted at and she was use to running the kitchen her own way. Moshe was a very talented chef in his own right who also knew what he wanted to accomplish and was well on his way to accomplishing that goal. It's been said before that too many cooks in the kitchen can spoil the broth. Soon, both cook's patients were beginning to show signs of breaking down as they began to fight and bicker over the evening meal preparation.

Unfortunately, this story ended in the wrong way. Sofia held her ground and insisted that Moshe leave the kitchen to her. Moshe was offended that his help was not wanted or accepted and decided to back out of the kitchen and eventually left the church. If this story sounds familiar to you, don't worry you are not alone. Many churches go through similar scenarios where feelings get hurt as people strive to hold their territories.

In Paul's letter to the Ephesians' church body he states in verse twelve of chapter six "For we do not wrestle against flesh and blood, but against principalities, against powers, against the rulers of the darkness of this age, against spiritual hosts of wickedness in the heavenly places." Ephesians 6:12 NKJV.

We are engaged in an unseen spiritual battle that rages on all around us. Because the nature of this battle is in the spiritual realm we cannot prosper by fighting it in the physical world by using our own flesh. In fact, that is our enemy's battle plan to get us to fight in the flesh where we are not using the arsenal of spiritual armor and weapons that God provides for our use.

Satan is our enemy; make no mistake about it. His battle plan has been tested and proven to be successful time and time again. He knows the weaknesses of human beings and that is where the front lines of this spiritual battle is taking place. His battle plan / strategy are to first divide us then conquer by tempting us to fight in the flesh.

When we lack unity in the Holy Spirit we are cut off from central command and wander around aimlessly; essentially being sidelined from the fight. Paul also advises us in chapter two, verse three "Do nothing from selfish ambition or conceit, but in humility count other more significant than yourselves. Let each of you look not only to his own interests, but also to the interests of others." Ephesians 2:3 NKJV.

Jesus, was quoted in the gospel of John, chapter seventeen, verse twenty-one "I do not ask for these only, but also for those who will believe in me through their word, that they may be one, just as you, Father, are in me, and I in you, that they may be in us, so that the world may believe that you have sent me." John 17:21 NKJV.

Jesus clearly lays out our battle plan for every person which is to be unified as one body in Christ. As long as we stay connected to the One True Vine then the Holy Spirit can continue to empower us through the battles of life. His unlimited power and resources is our greatest asset, however, we must remain in fellowship with one another to keep the sap flowing through the vine.

Like the effects of kryptonite on superman, the following list of wrong behaviors will sever us from God's arsenal essentially sidelining us from engaging in the battle: adultery, fornication, uncleanness, lewdness, idolatry, sorcery, hatred, contentions, jealousies, outbursts of wrath, selfish ambitions, dissensions, heresies, envy, murders, drunkenness, revelries and the like.

Many hands make the work easier so get others involved and remember that the battle belongs to the Lord. Stay in the battle by keeping unity within the fellowship and continue walking in the Holy Spirit.

The beach

My phone startled me as it vibrated against my leg and I watched another set of waves break against the shore. I usually don't answer my phone anymore if I don't recognize the number but today for some odd reason I swished my finger across the screen and accepted the call.

"Hello?" I asked which was followed by a moment of silence as if the caller knew I never answered my phone.

"Oh hi, this is Bella Knight, I am researching a story for a local paper. Do you have time to talk about a few details?"

It was quite a relief to discover that it wasn't another solar contractor, window replacement pitch or farm aid plea and that someone actually wanted to talk to me. She was friendly, motivated and I decided at that very moment I would do everything in my power to help dig up some useful information for my fellow journalist even if I had to make up it.

So far today was going exceptionally well as we were able to find a parking space near Law Street public beach access, several semi-clean, open bathroom stalls as well as a small patch of unclaimed sand that was surrounded by a mote of kelp. Sand flies attracted by the rotting kelp seemed to sense a better meal had arrived and immediately began to devour me from top to bottom.

Quickly I unfurled my fold-out sand chair, slathered myself with zinc oxide and sat down to begin a long stretch of "people watching". My wife had accompanied me and was busy getting her boogie board ready for the surf. She insists that my highly developed skill of "people watching" can really be condensed down to ogling young women in skimpy bikinis but that is just simply not true!

It is actually very enlightening to watch people at the beach as they engaged in activities that one would only do while running around half naked on the sand. Some of these activities probably resemble games Stone Age people played as they discovered sticks and round stones and began to bat them around on the ground.

Take paddleball for instance. Has anyone actually seen this game being played at home, in the park or at any other public place? Usually a typical paddleball scenario goes like this: player one hits rubber ball towards player two but the ball veers off and hits a total stranger who was sleeping stretched out on their towel. Player two says "Oh, I am so sorry" retrieves ball, blushes and returns volley in the direction of player one. The ball veers off again into the surf and on and on this ritual goes until player one gets tired or player two decides he is hungry.

Next on my list of favorite people watching skills is the appreciation of "body art" that is unabashingly displayed as one strips down to enjoy the ocean's shore. Now, just before I alienate a good portion of my younger readers it is a fact that my generation did not have the opportunity to enjoy organ piercings, body art or snot and lint catchers of any kind.

While sitting in my chair I soon became fascinated by some of the art I saw. Some designs were really quite beautiful being carefully positioned and originally created while others took on a sort of silk screen print image that one might duplicate a hundred times for a long line of unsuspecting customers.

The one I especially liked depicted a full set of angel wings from shoulders to waist. The design's dark rigid straight lines must have cost a fortune, been extremely painful and taken several weeks to complete. I'll stop to say that I am extremely grateful that no one has thought to reproduce Darth Maul on their face.

I will say this, in defense of all my unsuspecting victims, that at least they were doing something. Walking, running, playing, just having fun while I just spent my entire day at the beach just sitting covered from head to toe desperately trying to escape the fury of solar radiation. How pathetic is that? Right?

So let wisdom ring from the fool's choir and let us fully enjoy the life that God has granted us. Play paddleball, get body art and exercise to the fullest. Don't wake up someday at ninety-eight and realize that life has passed you by. Be kind to one another, esteeming others more worthy than yourself.

Take a deep and long breath only to let it out slowly. Smell several roses as you pass by while you allow their fragrance to elevate you to higher thought. Praise your Creator for how fearfully and wonderfully made you are. Admire swimwear and the all forms that fill them.

Cracked Cisterns

Water, the quintessential component of life, is so necessary that without it your body will begin to shut down after only four days. Our bodies are composed of sixty percent of it and every cell in our body needs it to continue the many processes that keep us alive.

The earth's massive oceans comprise over seventy percent of our planet's surface. They are not only a fertile source for food, our atmosphere's oxygen supply but also supply fresh water to our villages and communities. God's hydrological cycle begins by forming clouds through the process of evaporation that eventually and graciously deposit fresh water over the many mountain ranges on our continents.

Our oceans were designed as earth's buffering system to regulate many complex systems that keep all life flourishing. Unfortunately, the human race has used this precious resource to deposit their waste, allowed overfishing and radioactive material to contaminate them.

Many concerned scientists, environmental activists and citizens are troubled at the apparent lack of concern among all nations of the world. It is becoming very obvious that our ocean's delicate balance is being overloaded with pollution and may be reaching the tipping point of no return.

As the new industrial revolution continues to spiral out of control, the dumping of radioactive waste is being allowed to continue in countries around the world, the consequences will be catastrophic for all life on earth.

While the word picture I have just painted is indeed full of darkness and despair, unlike a Kinkade portrait which is filled with the hope and light, there is yet still hope. The redemption of mankind as well as the earth has already been accomplished and the curtain on the final act is about to go up for the last call.

The nation of Israel, all children from the twelve sons of Jacob, was commanded to worship only the One, True and Living God who is the Fountain of Living Water, the Well with the Holy Name.

Unfortunately, like all of us, the nation of Israel turned their backs on God and began to worship other contrived gods of heavenly and earthly origins. God's design, to use Jacob's children to reveal His plan of salvation to the entire world, was derailed as men allowed greed, power and lust to draw them away to the deception of false gods and idol worship.

"Be astonished, O heavens, at this, and be horribly afraid; be very desolate," says the Lord. For My people have committed two evils: They have forsaken Me, the fountain of living waters, and hewn themselves cisterns-broken cisterns that can hold no water." Jeremiah 2:13 NKJV.

This text, found in Jeremiah, lists two destructive acts committed not only by the nation of Israel but all humanity. The world has indeed turned their backs on the source of life and instead dug for themselves cisterns-broken cisterns, which cannot hold water.

Since the very beginning of creation God has promised that it would be Him who would correct the mistakes of mankind. His answer has always been the giving of Himself in the form of the Messiah or Savior to reverse the original generational curse on mankind.

God sent His only begotten Son into the world to purchase mankind out of slavery. How did God accomplish this? God chose to send Himself into our world, to be born of a virgin, live a life free from sin, which then paid the ultimate price to redeem us all.

Jeshua once told a Samaritan women, who was sitting with Him nearby a well, that He was the source of Living Water. If she drank water from Jacob's well she would thirst again but if she drank from the Well with the Holy Name she would never thirst again and live forever.

As the final curtain is being drawn up, the trumpet sounded and an end comes to the two thousand year old intermission, all who receive God's free gift of salvation are about to be redeemed and restored. Your destiny, as well as the destiny of all your family and friends, rests solely on the act of asking to receive the Living Water from God's Fountain.

However, our lives are like cracked cisterns that cannot hold water as we continue to forsake God and dig cisterns of our own making which cannot hold the Holy Spirit. Today is your divine appointment; do not wait for a human solution by attempting to fill the cracked cistern of your own making. Chose Jesus, the Living Water of life and live forever by coming to the Well with the Holy Name.

"And the Spirit and the bride say, Come! And let him who hears say, Come! And let him who thirsts come. Whoever desires, let him take the water of life freely." Revelation 22:17 NKJV.

Seeds of faith

Its 2:22 on Tuesday afternoon as I walk out my front door my Terrier-Border collie mix meets me with her favorite Frisbee in her mouth. I grab it and sail it through the air past a courtyard full of roses, iris, geraniums and star jasmine. She misses catching it because it was a bad throw and the disc careens into a large Dandelion patch. Several of the spherical seeds explode into the air sending hundreds of parachute like seeds on a new journey in search of a place to sprout and grow.

I turn back to look and catch a sweet fragrance of the star jasmine which is in full bloom. Thousands of tiny star pointed blossoms release their perfume-like aroma into the gentle breeze that meanders through the confines of the courtyard. A ruby throated hummingbird joins me as we both enjoy pushing our faces into the hedge of jasmine. Below me beautifully robed Easter irises parade their purple patterned flower attire down the garden runway. I accidentally bump into a climbing Cecile Brunet rose bush that is dotted every few inches with tightly furrowed rose buds that compete with the jasmine for first place in the fragrance category.

I pause to listen to a peregrine falcon as it silently but swiftly navigate through a rose arbor in pursuit of a darting sparrow that is determined to get away. A pair of brightly colored yellow oriels perch in the weeping wisteria watching the entire spectacle relieved that the falcon wasn't chasing after them. Nearby several Humming birds jockey for nectar that has been carefully placed out in a feeder hanging on a nearby pine tree. As I survey the colossal pine a cone randomly topples down releasing several seeds that helicopter down to the ground.

It's just amazing to me to see all this design, sacred geometry, which our Creator has built into our world. The dandelion's spherical shape allows the wind from any direction to lift the parachute shaped seeds high into the air where they will be dispersed to another location. Once there, if they find sun, water and soil then they will sprout and grow. The pine seeds, in a different way, have one lop sided wing that causes them to spiral out and away from their parent tree where by enabling them to find sun, water and soil to grow in.

The flowers too have aromas and colors that attract insects that will do the work of pollination. In fact flowers have color wavelengths that are beyond our visible spectrum but not to specific insects that search them out. These colors can be compared to and are the equivalent of the neon signs that beckon us to enter a storefront when it is open. All these incredible proofs of God's existence and design were observed only fifteen feet from my front door.

Spring is a wonderful time to watch the sap rise in the trees, flowers bloom and what was once thought of as dead comes back to life. It was during this same time of year that Jesus prophesied "The hour has come that the Son of Man should be glorified. Most assuredly, I say to you, unless a grain of wheat falls into the ground and dies, it remains alone; but if it dies, it produces much grain." John 12:23,24 NKJV.

Jesus fulfilled numerous prophecies as He rode into Jerusalem presenting Himself as the world's final Passover Lamb. Then at the last supper He made a New Covenant, in His blood, where He invited all to dine at His table and to remember not only His sacrifice on the cross but that he rose from the dead.

The message of Easter is "Christ is Risen!" It's a message of life for all to share who come to dine at Christ's table. Creation even sings its songs to our Heavenly Father and refocuses our minds on the glorious things that are in store for us in heaven. The purple of the flowering iris and the sweet aroma of jasmine remind us that death has no longer any hold on us and that Jesus Christ has taken away the sting of death forever. It's a time to rejoice, sing, jump and cry out to God for the wonderful love He has for us.

Easter is so much more than bunny rabbits and colored eggs. Baskets overflowing with candy don't come close to the sweetness that Christ has in store for us. We are the apple of His eye and He faithfully loves every single person He has created. So in the end, Jesus became as that grain of wheat that died then came back to life to produce much grain. Creation declares the glory of God and stands as a witness of His overflowing bountiful goodness.

Sky car

Its Sunday evening late in the fall of 1963 and the newest episode of the my favorite space cartoon about an outer space family is about to premiere. For you younger space travelers the cartoon depicted a family who lived in a floating city where robotic maids cleaned and cooked for them making their lives incredibly more endurable. The citizens of earth also navigated the heavens by flying in space age sky cars which defied gravity. Life was incredibly trouble free in this modern utopia.

I want to take a closer look at these sky cars. Yes, believe it or not they are going to be an everyday sight that will eventually fill the skies in which are now crowed with large air busses. These space age cars, operated by globally positioned satellites, will give humans the freedom to get anywhere without the hands of a human driver and without the possibility of accident or loss of human life.

Now I want you to consider something. Let's look at how wonderfully vast our universe is and one illuminating component we call light. If light travels at 186,000 miles at second then it will take light particles leaving the surface of the sun about 8.4 minutes to reach earth. To give you a perspective that is closer to earth think about this; in the time it takes you to flip on a light switch, light would have already traveled 7.4 times around the circumference of the earth at the equator. Now, it took me 2 days in the air just to fly just halfway around the world to Kathmandu in a jumbo jet flying at 450 miles an hour.

Let me develop this idea a little further to illustrate a future point. Our solar system is located in one of several spiral arms of the Milky Way galaxy. The closest star to us is Proxima Centauri at 4.2 light years from earth. That is the distance that light travels in 4.2 years at a speed of 186,000 miles per second. To put this in laymen's terms, that's a long way. If we launched a probe it would take 20,000 years to reach it.

Let's take one additional cosmic step before settling back down to terra firma. It's roughly estimated that our galaxy contains 300 billion stars. Its diameter is 100,000 light years across, remember that light can circle our globe 7.4 times in a second and light would have to travel for 100,000 years to travel the diameter of our own galaxy. Yikes!

Now let's look at psalm 19. "The heavens declare the glory of God; and the firmament shows His handiwork. Day unto day utters speech, and night unto night reveals knowledge. There is no speech nor language where their voice is not heard. Their line has gone out through all the earth and their words to the end of the world. In them He has set a tabernacle for the sun, which is like a bridegroom coming out of his chamber, and rejoices like a strong man to run its race. Its rising is from one end of heaven, and its circuit to the other end; and there is nothing hidden from its heat. The law of the Lord is perfect, converting the soul; The testimony of the Lord is sure, making wise the simple; The statutes of the Lord are right, rejoicing the heart; The commandment of the Lord is pure, enlightening the eyes; The fear of the Lord is clean, enduring forever; The judgments of the Lord are true and righteous altogether. More to be desired are they than gold, Yea, than much fine gold; Sweeter also than honey and the honeycomb. Moreover by them Your servant is warned, and in keeping them there is great reward. Who can understand his errors? Cleanse me from secret faults. Keep back Your servant also from presumptuous sins; Let them not have dominion over me. Then I shall be blameless, and I shall be innocent of great transgression. Let the words of my mouth and the meditation of my heart be acceptable in Your sight, O Lord, my strength and my Redeemer." Psalm 19 NKJV.

Is it really that hard to believe in God? The obvious precision in which the heavenly bodies operate shows that there is design to the overall operation of the universe in which we live. If there is design then there is a designer and suddenly all of our problems that look like mountains here on earth begin to shrink into the microscopic world as we jump into our sky cars and head out into the heavens! The heavens certainly do declare the glory of God.

Sweet fragrance

Pastor Doug was running late as always as the line at the bank drive-thru began to lurch forward. He had to make a deposit for the church, speed home to eat dinner then back out on the road to make a pastoral visit at a local Hospital. Even though the bank's drive thru were three lanes wide it was Friday and everyone was making deposits before the weekend.

Pulling up to the vacuum tube equipped kiosk Doug sorted through fifty checks making sure that they had the church's endorsement stamped on the back. He then made sure they were right side up before inserting them into the plastic capsule. The capsule made a slurp, whooshing sound as it disappeared down the tube. Several minutes later Doug heard the voice of a young girl asking "Sir, I'm sorry but I have to ask you a question?"

Doug paused to remember if he had indeed signed all the checks, included the cash or had forgotten the deposit slip? The girls' voice reappeared. "Can you tell me the name of the fragrance you are wearing?" Puzzled, Doug remembered that he must have had some remnant of Old Spice left on his hands from this morning's shave. The left over fragrance had been transferred to the checks while he sorted them into the capsule and that aroma had traveled all the way over to the teller behind the bullet proof glass.

Kenny took the city bus everywhere. This morning he had an early appointment at the library where he was applying for a clerk's position sorting through books. As he stepped off of the bus he caught a whiff of something wonderful in the air but it was fleeting and soon replaced with the foul smell of the bus's diesel engines.

The walking green illuminated as Kenny rounded the corner of Main Street. As he strides past the laundry mat the smell of fresh, clean clothes poured out through the open double doors of the laundry mat reminding him it was wash day. Half way down Main Street Kenny smelled the same heavenly aroma that he had briefly enjoyed when he had first stepped off the bus.

It made him think of apple pies, bagels, donuts and freshly baked bread. Soon he came to the bakery and watched as the baker removed a loaf of freshly baked bread from a wood fired oven. He started to salivate, forgot all about his appointment at the library and turned into the shop to buy a slice of fresh apple pie.

Paul penned "Now thanks be to God who always leads us in triumph in Christ, and through us diffuses the fragrance of His knowledge in every place." 2 Corinthians 2:14 NKJV.

Beautiful fragrances can remind us of people in our lives, they can cause us to turn into a bakery or be attracted to someone. Sweet smelling aromas of orange blossoms, star jasmine and freshly baked bread are wonderful and put a smile on our faces. There are also foul odorous aromas that repel us and cause us to turn and walk away in disgust.

The apostle Paul wrote "You are our epistle written in our hearts, known and read by all men; clearly you are an epistle of Christ, ministered by us, written not with ink but by the Spirit of the living God, not on tablets of stone but on tablets of flesh, that is, of the heart." 2 Corinthians 3:2 NKJV.

We represent Jesus Christ everywhere we go in our lives and during the course of each day. For many, we will be the only bible people will ever read.

We are to be sweet smelling aromas by diffusing love, joy, peace, kindness, generosity, gentleness, goodness and self control to the people around us. People should be drawn to us because of our aroma of kindness asking "How can I get what you have?"

Unfortunately, many of us have foul aromas that repel people from wanting to know more about God. We demand too much of people living by the letter of the law rather than by the Spirit. Many times we as Christians cause strife, dissentions and contentions because of our selfish ambitions. It might be our drunkenness, out bursts of wrath, an unkind word or even just participating in gossip that causes strife in our families and churches.

What we need is a daily, supernatural re-filling of the Holy Spirit in order to love and be kind to others as we diffuse the sweet smelling aroma of Jesus Christ. "Therefore be imitators of God as dear children. And walk in love, as Christ also has loved us and given Himself for us, an offering and a sacrifice to God for a sweet smelling aroma."

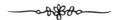

Bond Servants

Demetrius begged his owner "I just want to be your bond servant. I give back my freedom, my freewill to you; please allow me to serve you all the days of my life!"

Titus was extremely fond of Demetrius and over the years he had become like part of his family. As the jubilee was fast approaching he had looked forward to giving Demetrius back his freedom. Demetrius was born in Corinth and was captured in a border war seven years earlier in the northern territories. He was one of the lucky ones who had been well treated by his master and wanted to remain as a house servant.

"Please allow me to stay with your family. Put a ring through my ear and I will serve you all the days the Lord has granted me." said Demetrius as he set down the tray holding this morning's sweet honeysuckle, tea and flatbread.

Titus smiled as the request of his servant resonated through the quiet morning air. He smiled and instructed Demetrius to find a hammer and awl while he retrieved a gold ring from the house's strong box. Titus gently placed Demetrius' ear onto the doorpost of his home as the awl was driven through his earlobe with one smooth swing of the hammer.

Titus inserted the gold ring through the hole he had just made and closed the ring with another quick swing. Martha, one of the other housemaids, quickly and tenderly anointed the wound with virgin olive oil as Titus ordered the entire house to prepare for a celebration!

This short word picture of a grateful slave and a kind master is not so different from the relationship that all Christians should have with Jesus Christ. We were all once lost in the world's battles, captured by the enemy and bound, fettered to the sins of our old life.

Jesus, our Lord and Master, has graciously invited us to receive freedom from the bondage of our old life that so easily ensnares us. As we accept His gift of forgiveness we are taken out of the world through our new birth and then allowed to make a conscious choice to be obedient to our Master or continue living in bondage.

Just as the nation of Israel stood on the east side of the Jordan River looking out over at the Promised Land, we too must decide what we will do with our new found freedom. God was giving them Canaan and all they had to do was to be obedient to their Master and totally posses it. However, they decided not to totally trust in God and failed to occupy the entire land they were promised.

We too have entered the resurrected land of freedom in Christ and have access to all the blessings and promises that come with it if we will obediently occupy God's sovereign territory. Living for Christ means to become a bond servant and to willing give back our rights, our freedom in order to serve our Master. In this way we will possess the entire resurrected life promised to us by God.

Because we have freewill, we must either continue to live selfish lives that only serve our flesh or surrender our lives to our Lord to be set apart for only His glory. The choice is ours; to become bond servants or to continue to serve other idols and gods.

Today can be our day of jubilee where we make that choice to follow Him! Our first step is to begin by surrendering our secret places, thoughts and habits to the Holy Spirit. Through His power we can become free from the chains that bind us to our flesh. In this way we are not only entering the Promised Land but also occupying every promise that has been prepared for us.

In our story, Demetrius was so grateful for his Master's love and kindness that he made the choice to give back his freedom and serve his Master for life. In the same way, it is God's kindness that leads us to repentance and a life that is truly holy, set apart and pure.

Repentance is a fruit, a gift of the Spirit which only grows as we continue to stay connected to the True Vine. Jesus is the vine and we are the branches. Don't be discouraged when pruning season arrives as it is a necessity in order for us to bear much fruit. If we could repent in our power and strength by living perfect lives then we wouldn't have any need of a Savior?

God loves us and that is why He sent His own Son into the world to purchase us out of slavery to sin. Be set free today and drink from the Living Water.

"Be set free today and drink from the Living Water."

Printed in the United States
By Bookmasters